BLUEBERRIES

Ellena Savage is an Australian author and academic. She is the author of the chapbook *Yellow City* (The Atlas Review, 2019) and numerous essays, stories, and poems published in literary journals internationally. Ellena is the recipient of several grants and fellowships, including most recently the Marten Bequest Travelling Scholarship 2019–2021. She lives in Athens, Greece, with her husband, Dominic Amerena.

ELLENA SAVAGE

BLUEBERRIES

essays concerning
understanding

SCRIBE
Melbourne • London

Scribe Publications
2 John St, Clerkenwell, London, WC1N 2ES, United Kingdom

Published in conjunction with Text Publishing of Melbourne, Australia
This edition published by Scribe 2020
Reprinted 2021

Some of these essays have appeared elsewhere, in slightly or very different
form: 'Yellow City' in *Paris Review Daily*, November 2018; 'Satellite' in
Chart Collective: Legend, 2017; 'Allen Ginsberg' in *Scum Magazine*, October
2017; 'Unwed Teen Mum Mary' in *Choice Words*, Allen & Unwin, 2019;
'You Dirty Phony Saint and Martyr' in the *Lifted Brow* No. 32, December
2016 (and shortly afterwards republished online in *Literary Hub*);
'Friendship Between Women' in *Cosmonaut's Avenue*, August 2018;
'The Literature of Sadness' in the *Lifted Brow* No. 33, March 2017;
'Turning Thirty' in the *Lifted Brow Online*, December 2017. The titles
'Holidays with Men' and 'Antimemoir, as in, Fuck You (as in, Fuck Me)' are
taken from pieces previously published in, respectively, the *Suburban Review*
Vol. 1, 2013, and the *Lifted Brow* No. 35, September 2017. Some lines and
observations in this book have appeared, unedited, in the self-published,
closed-circuit weekly email newsletter *Little Throbs*.

Excerpt from *Don't Let Me Be Lonely: An American Lyric* by Claudia
Rankine (Penguin Books 2017) Copyright © Claudia Rankine, 2017

Typeset by Jessica Horrocks & Duncan Blachford

Printed and bound in the UK by CPI Group (UK) Ltd, Croydon CR0 4YY

Scribe is committed to the sustainable use of natural resources and the use
of paper products made responsibly from those resources.

978 1 912854 67 7 (paperback)
978 1 925938 18 0 (ebook)

Catalogue records for this book are available from the British Library.

scribepublications.co.uk

For Dominic.

Yellow City

1 February 2017

A worn-out black turtleneck, skin-tight black jeans. The same clothes I wore when I travelled here alone, eleven years ago. I notice this only while sitting in the back seat of the taxi into Lisbon with Dom. Now, however, I am one-and-a-half dress sizes larger. Now, my jeans are tailored and my sweater has a designer label. Now, I don't wear whimsical fur-collared coats or charming hats from the 1920s to suggest the possibility that I am interesting.

The last time I came to Lisbon, eleven years ago, I could talk to any person in the world. I had fast learned how to sleep in any number of positions: between the farts and fucks and snores of adolescent adults in hostels; on a row of couch cushions laid out by earnest Belgian students on their Erasmus year; with my head resting on the shoulder of a fleshy Brazilian on an overnight bus. I saw no problem in taking time from others, or accepting their hospitality, because I was paying it forward. I was a general, all-purpose, adaptable person. All my unrealised potential suggested that I might become exactly like any one of the people I encountered.

>—*In becoming specific, narrower, more difficult, you, you don't have much left to give.*

>—But it's true. We dress the same, she and I. And we didn't get any better.

2 February 2017

This is where it began. Lisbon, May 2006. Outside the club at the Santo Amaro docks, I dangled my legs over the edge of the wide river, my feet swinging like a purse at the end of a long strap. Above me, Lisbon's big bridge, red and hung, just like the Golden Gate. I puffed smoke into the air excessively, the way I always do on long boozy nights, though I hadn't had a drink for a couple of hours.

>—She's lying.

I drank water from a flimsy plastic bottle!

>—*Or vodka lime soda? Though you might still have been on your caipirinha bent, after Coimbra.*

The girl I had gone to the club with, the woman, was kissing her new man inside while I waited. They had brought me here, in his car, from the bar with pink fairy lights that he owned in the Bairro Alto.

The woman with whom I had come was a stray I had 'saved' several hours earlier. She was walking, alone, with a brawny shadow behind her. Locking eyes with me, she called out, 'It's so good to see you!'

'It's good to see you, too,' I replied. Like that, I rescued her from a man who might have hurt her. We struck up a conversation. We kept it going. Later, she said, 'I'm going to meet a friend; would you like to come?'

>—She might have helped the woman find a cab.

>—*It was just a twenty-minute walk. And the glorious amber of Lisbon at night.*

It's true—others were with us. To celebrate the woman's escape, we stepped into a bar that smelled of yeast and bought a round of frothy beers. Her hair was long and wavy and she laughed at all my jokes. She was smaller than me and more beautiful. I *wanted* to follow her.

>—*A night opens up. Who are you to say no to it?*

>—Don't go.

>—*Too late.*

The man she was kissing inside the club was in possession of a figure that didn't support his gut. Tall and fine-boned, he would have been slim but for the soft pouch of his belly, his hangdog chin. I couldn't imagine what my new friend saw in him.

>—*Why had she not chosen you?*

But then, I was fresh out of high school. What did I know about sex? Sitting by the river I talked loud-mouthedly to two young men, nineteen-year-olds with faces they'd one day grow into. Lit with vexation,

>—The woman with wavy hair had dropped her.

I endeavoured to make my own way through the night. Conversation unfurled between the two young guys and me as we shared a diminishing supply of cigarettes.

I was on a break from school, working in bars and maxing out my credit cards for the privilege of seeing a world that wasn't mine. I was enrolled in a law degree, which I was to start the following year (which I never did). Law, of all things.

>—No more second-hand bedsheets.

>—*You thought you could evade me.*

>—Her feeling of entitlement, of significance, not yet
>knowing that it doesn't come.

The boys with callow faces, were they business students? They longed to visit Australia. We swapped email addresses, just as I had swapped them, dropped them, in every city I stepped through. Did anyone ever email? Yes. But only the boys who thought I'd come with them to Corsica.

>—*The Corsicans were the worst.*

It was light, now. I looked across the Tagus at the harsh stare of Jesus, Christ the King, the grand monument, arms outstretched from the mountaintop across the river. Christ the King, installed there by the fascist government, was in no position, I thought, to judge me. The boys promised me breakfast, the best *pastel de Belém* in Belém. I accepted. I went to say goodbye to my new friend. She told me not to go with them.

　　—She was right to sense danger.

　　　—*Did she think that instead you'd go back with her, to his place? Watch them screw?*

Just one chance. One more in a series of chances that had led me to her, to this.

I'll go with them, I said. It's fine. I'm a big girl. The woman with long wavy hair wrote her number on a piece of card that I slipped into a fold in my wallet.

　　—*You didn't have a phone.*

3 February 2017

When I am asked what the first news story I remember is—and because I cannot organise my memories in such a way—I say Princess Di. Other people my age say this, and so it has become my first news memory, too. Though it may have to do with the film *Amélie*, which romanticises the princess-death. The Thredbo disaster was a month earlier, however, and I remember that perfectly. I was nine.

She, the blonde princess, didn't mean all that much to me, and so in her death I didn't lose anything personal except perhaps a belief in the myth that blonde princesses live happily ever after. What I gained instead was a sensation of hot metal folding into my body, of boiling black oil spilling over my arms and face. Unlike the funerals of elderly family members, their peaceful

5

grey bodies packaged smartly in timber boxes, Princess Diana, *Lady Die*, gave me the flesh knowledge of violent death. A useful memory to hold within your skin, as any one of us might take our last breath in a state of absolute terror.

Today I will call the police. I mean, I will call the 'tourist police', who take down tourists' statements on official stationery and stamp them, so that tourists may claim the value of their stolen purses with their travel insurance companies. When I last came into contact with Lisbon's tourist police, eleven years ago, I had to wait for an hour against a wall lined with orange plastic chairs— or maybe they were blue?—as an endless parade of dusty-haired English and French couples reported acts of petty theft against them. I was there to report an almost-rape.

> *—A sexual assault?*

An encounter during which my flesh remembered the possibility of a violent death. When my body understood for a second that corpses are dismembered to cover up crimes. By kicking and screaming and running, I had got away from the death, so what was there to report?

> —An attempt.

> *—A terror.*

> —A scare.

Waiting for the tourist police then, eleven years ago, my organs felt heavy from the no-sleep, from the trauma, from the traces of alcohol still left in my blood. But I was chipper and businesslike. I buried my shame deep alongside my fear, and I gave my statement, describing how two young men had conspired to rape me and almost succeeded, but I weaselled my way out by agreeing to other acts of violence, and then by my hysteria, and then by my physical desperation to flee. I was so chipper that, once I'd finished and signed my statement, the tourist policeman wrote his number on a piece of paper and said, 'I finish at ten—let me take you out and show you the *real* Lisbon.'

4 February 2017

I didn't call the tourist police yesterday; today, Saturday, the office is closed. This might have been unconscious, an avoidance.

> *—Or, lazy?*

> —Un-pleasure avoidance through pleasure? She wouldn't go that far.

I'm not in the habit of living by Freud, but I admit that he has given me useful words to sort through my actions. I knew, for example, that I would come to Lisbon to find a copy of the police investigation; I knew that for many months. I knew, too, that I'd be searching for the documents that detail, in some kind of truth of their time, what happened to me, eleven years ago. But now that I'm here, I can't even pick up the phone. I don't want to know.

> *—But you do.*

> —She doesn't want to know the words she gave that tourist police officer, so revealing will they be of what essence she's made.

> *—Were made of then, which makes you now, no threshold between you.*

I know what the pleasure principle is: it is not calling up the tourist police when I intend to. It is preserving the self that I am used to living with and going to great lengths to protect it from disruptions. Freud's exact words won't assist me here unless I've already been living by them.

Instead, I've been living with the detritus of pop psychology, like:

+ Strength can be willed.

+ Fear can be conquered.

+ It's not difficult to be truthful.

The idea that 'confronting demons' is, firstly, possible, and, secondly, a good idea.

5 February 2017

—One can only conceptualise memory through metaphor. A sieve a warehouse an attic a skeleton a cupboard a filing system a database a basement an encyclopaedia a landscape a dustbin a grab bag. A tape recorder. RAM. A cathedral.

—Memory is the scribe of the soul. (Aristotle)

—*That's romantic—ergo, bullshit.*

—Memory is a reconstructive process. (Cognitive Behavioural Therapy)

—Or in the living arena of speech, memory is idiomatic. _____ like an elephant tripping down _____ lane jogging your _____ commit it to

_____ a living _____ know it by _____ allow me to refresh your _____.

—If memory is not a tape recorder starting at zero, then how can a self exist, truly?

—To attach to memory some order, an architecture, helps assuage the sense that one has slipped into a warm pond, only to turn around and find oneself in treacherous waters, far from land.

—Anchor memories to signposts that suggest linear time. How old was I then. What was my mother doing. I was a size eight. Tony Moretti loved me.

—'My first memory.'

—Is buttressed by recalling it.

—'My first memory.' A fiction fixed to the linear self.

—If only to survive the terror of selflessness.

—But I remember mine. My first memory, Paula, an artist at the residency, said. I was three, and I remember thinking, 'I'm not so young anymore. I'm three.'

—'Her first memory.' It was pink pink pink. And red, peach light, close-up mottled black. Eyelids stuck pressed shut pressed against the breast. Vitreous fluid moves against. Breast. The muted sound of booming voices, dense. Everything thick all wet velvet dusky stuck together.

—Time precedes you. A framework for the private self, totally. Alone.

—'And yet the image we have of ourselves is mediated through the other. Indeed, it is only the other who can see us, as it were, "objectively".' (Hans Ruin)

—'It takes two to witness the unconscious.' (Freud, via Shoshana Felman)

—Does trauma need a witness? If it does, you'll need to have this published. Or else you will be your only witness.

6 February 2017 (Absolutely no meaning whatsoever)

Polícia de Segurança Pública.

Olá. Hi. Do you speak English?

Yes.

I have a strange request. In 2006, I was the victim of a crime in Lisbon, and it went to court, but I had to leave Portugal before I was able to find out what happened, so I'd like to see if I can track down the documents from this time.

Okay, so it was eleven years ago. So the problem is, eleven years later our paper has absolutely no meaning whatsoever.

What…does that mean.

It means the situation was a long time ago and the situation is in the archives; it has been archived for ten years.

Is it possible to access the file from the archives? I don't intend to pursue the matter at all, I just want to read it.

I can print it for you, but it has absolutely no meaning. If you want, you can send an email to the police. The situation is that we don't give the police report in email.

Can I come in person? I'm here in Lisbon.

Okay, you can come here. Bring your ID.

7 February 2017 (A bad day)

Sometimes I think it's possible to live with anything. That we're wired to survive-survive-survive, to grip onto the gnarliest thread until life is pried from our bones. Other times I think it's not possible to live at all. Not at all.

> —*Is that how you preface a flurry of complaints?*

> —A knuckle clenched in her gut.

After phoning the tourist police, we—Dom and I—walk to a police station near our building. But Dom has the address wrong in his phone and, with no internet, we wander round like puppies, following indecipherable directions given to us by fruiterers. Each time we turn a corner, one of his work boots crunches down on my much smaller foot, by accident.

> —*Found it.*

I explain 'the situation' to a group of eight male officers in severe boots, military haircuts. None of them speak English.

> —*They sent you home!*

—To another station, downtown.

—*The sun was miraculous in the sky.*

—Tomorrow. Her breasts are heavy today, back aching.

We stop to rest in our room before heading to the other station. Once back at the studio, lethargy takes over. In bed, I listen to an audiobook history of the Salem witch trials. *Unbelievable!* I think, and then, *somewhat believable*—the madness of myth and misogyny and violence. I laugh, then, at the absurdity. These girls, swaying and chanting with the viral madness that possessed them. The men's horror at the collapse of their neutral, natural power.

—The blanket beneath her legs is hot and dry in the sun. Her insides throb, but the blood does not arrive.

The artist residency we are staying at is highly disorganised. We don't have a stovetop in the studio, we don't have a key to the communal kitchen downstairs. In the cupboard, there is one butter knife, two bowls, two forks. A chopping board. A microwave on the bench. For these first few days, I cooked pasta in the microwave, which I then used to boil canned tomatoes with a clove of garlic (not recommended).

The air in our room is damp and it smells like the sea.

—*You don't want to read the police report.*

—But she is itchy all over. In the legs. Itchy in the shoulder blades.

After building up some guts again, we embark on the second journey downtown. Once there, I explain myself again. The man at the desk prints off the information he finds, the initial report I made in 2006. He sends me to another location, the Polícia Judiciária, an enormous, modern building bustling with detectives who are investigating serious crimes such as attempted rape.

At the Polícia Judiciária I explain to six, seven, eight more people 'the situation'. Finally, someone seems to know what I am after. The report. The file. The verdict of the trial that I never found out. I am told to wait.

Dom reaches for my hand and holds it lovingly, devotedly, as every cell in my body buzzes.

'Don't,' I say to Dom, shrugging off his love, trying to settle my hands down. 'Sorry. Just…frustrated.'

Hundreds of thickset detectives with charcoal overcoats and leather shoes cut out of the building for their lunch break. The lobby, wide and open as a gallery, is left empty.

Eventually, a middle-aged female detective, Cristina, comes out to explain that I will need to call yet another department. And that there will be a different reference number for my case after all—my name was incorrectly spelled in the initial report.

Back home in bed, bathed in sunlight, I turn the initial police report over in my hands. The names of the accused are written on the initial report. 'Tomas da Silva' and 'Salvator'.

Later, we eat the dreary pasta dinner and I sip my glass of wine too quickly. I pour another. A melodramatic, drunken thought crosses my mind: I'm not safe. I've never been safe.

—Which is probably, technically, true.

8 February 2017 (Are you afraid?)

What does a man become in the eleven years since he threw a girl's sense of being into chaos? This is the question I ask when I type 'Tomas da Silva' into Google. According to my yield, Tomas da Silva is a football hooligan. Tomas da Silva is also a yogi. He is a newlywed. He might be a mathematics professor in a woollen vest. Or a handsome Californian. A Miles Davis fan. An MBA graduate looking for work. A stocky young dad pleased with his brood. A professional soccer player who played for Benfica 1939–42. A helicopter pilot. A sappy boyfriend. A self-promoting guru. A surfer. A guy in aviators you'd avoid at a bar. A priest. A singer in a straw hat, laughing. A supply-chain manager. A teenage boy aware, and proud, of his burly new chest. A hotel manager with a sweet, plump fiancée. An acquisitions manager who has the look of a murderer. A seventeenth-century author of books that I determine are about Portuguese court life.

—Eleven years is a long time.

There is also the leader of 'People's Youth', a right-wing Christian lobby group whose purpose seems only to suppress same-sex marriage and abortion. This Tomas looks so familiar that I swear it is him, until I swear it is not, until I look at his features more closely and remember that dark brown hair, pale skin with spots, a nose on the larger, rounder side, and about *this tall*, is not enough to go on. And while it might have been droll, or something grimly related to it, in this case I am unable to name a Christian lobbyist a sex offender.

—*So you know their names, now, like you never forgot. Or maybe you're confusing them?*

—But Tomas is not the one she is afraid of.

You know when life is literary?

>—Dreams organised neatly into themes. Memories of childhood retold to fit with object-relation theory.

>—*Stretch it. And it fits.*

Well, the way I remember it,

>—*Or, you don't,*

Tomas is pale and Salvator is tanned. Tomas is round-nosed, Salvator is pointed. Tomas is soft-willed, Salvator, calculated.

Tomas is a garden-variety coward. Salvator is a literary psychopath.

>—*Neat.*

>—A dichotomy assists comprehension.

>—*For children and their moral equals.*

>—A dichotomy is usually false.

In court, in 2006, before I left Portugal, the boys' lawyers were each allowed to ask me a question. Tomas's lawyer asked me if I thought that his client was sorry for what he'd done. 'Yes,' I said, knowing that this was true. He was, I believed, horrified by what he had done.

Salvator's lawyer asked me if it was true that I'd said, before his client took me to an apartment, locked me in a room and pinned me down with the intention to rape me, 'Take me home and I'll fuck you'?

I leapt up in my chair like a cat. 'No! No, that's not true. No, I've never said that to anyone.' Which was true. I had never even thought of that constellation of words as my own.

While it was Tomas's cowardice that got me into that room that morning, it was his cowardice that got me out, too. As I literally, literarily, kicked and screamed under the boys' weight, heaving-crying and thinking that I would die, I desperately repeated, *I'll do anything, just please don't hurt me*.

　　　—I'll do anything, just please don't hurt me.

Tomas lost his cool. He burst into tears and rolled off the bed. And it was suddenly clear to Salvator that he couldn't handle the rape on his own. And Salvator said, 'Two blow jobs then! You can leave when you give us two blow jobs!' And I repeated the mantra *I'll do anything, just please don't hurt me*. And Tomas continued to cry and shouted at Salvator in Portuguese. And Salvator shouted, 'You're not leaving.' And I found my shirt and my skirt and my shoes and I bundled them up in my arms. And Salvator and Tomas screamed at one another. And I pulled some of my clothes on. And Tomas said to me, 'Come on.' And I moved towards the door. And Tomas made as if to open it. And we, one of us, opened it. And Salvator slammed his arm between it and me, and he said, 'Are you afraid?' And that's how I know he is a psychopath.

9 February 2017

On 7 June 2006, my older brother emailed me.

> Hey a letter from the portuguese sexual crimes bureau came in today, so I'm emailing to make sure you're ok?

I responded:

> Yes, I'm fine, I had a scare one night and took it very VERY seriously, and thus put two potential sex criminals in gaol. Well, not in gaol, but they're going to trial in the next few months. Don't tell Mum and Dad, they don't need to worry about anything.
>
> It was a pretty stressful situation, involving multiple trips to the police station and ID line-ups...But it's all over and despite the fact that it has come down to my word against theirs (and they have lawyers and will actually be present at the trial whereas only my statement will be present), I feel that in some small way, the fact that I followed it through and found them, and their families and friends now know, that a small amount of justice has been served.
>
> Apart from all that, I'm fine and dandy. I'm in Granada now which is very very beautiful. You'd love it.

I mean. Who speaks like that?

> —*Eighteen-year-old you, is who.*

>> Eighteen-year-old me, who will not let this ruin her trip! Who has exhausted her legal duties and will demand no concern,

> —*A small amount of justice has been served.*

>> who can absolutely handle trivial things like ID line-ups and slut-shaming lawyers, by herself, in a foreign land,

17

—Fine and dandy.

> whose parents need not be informed lest
> they ruin her new life, her new life that
> is, for the first time, her own.

—But it's all over…

If you wanted to phone home in 2006, you first had to go to a
tobacco stand or a deli and purchase a calling card, ten euros, and
scratch the silver film off the back of it with a coin, and find a
public phone, and dial the calling card company's phone number
followed by a long PIN, followed by the country code and then the
number you actually wanted to dial. Occasionally the call lasted as
long as it was supposed to, but usually the line would drop out and
you'd dial again, all those numbers, only to hear a pre-recorded
Portuguese woman inform you that you'd run out of credit.

I was always (and am still) in trouble for not calling, or emailing,
or visiting home often enough.

—Selfish.

Like many children—and who is not a child—I always felt a
fierce need to protect my inner life and even my public decisions
from my parents. I fear their intrusions and their judgements.
When I see them, I brace myself for the impending commentary
on the architecture of my life. I even brace myself for their love
and praise, because who knows what ghosts parental love might
awaken. As a daughter, I don't ask for help, and I know better
than to ask for validation. I don't reveal my darkest worries.
What I feel for them is love and duty. I help out when I can. And
in return for being low-needs, I ask for freedom.

—As if a parent could ever give that to their child.

In the middle of the 'fine and dandy it's just a minor sex crime' period, I called Mum and wept into the phone. I said, 'I love you', which was more demonstrative of me than usual. She said she loved me too, and begged me to tell her what was wrong. I said nothing specific, homesickness, maybe. Because I *was* fine, in a way. I was having the most thrilling most brightly lit time I had ever had. Everything, other than the minor-major sex crime, was fine, fine and dandy.

After I returned home to Melbourne, laden with debt, my father told me in a reproachful way that Mum had cried every night I had been gone—eight months or nine.

—A horrible thing for a child to be told.

—*As if it were possible for a daughter to give her mother freedom from maternal love.*

10 February 2017

Every time I garner the courage to call the prosecutor's number, the office that has access to my file, something intervenes. My Skype app automatically updates itself. The internet drops out. The receptionist can't understand me and hangs up. I try the other number, the number that Cristina gave me in case I needed to reach her, and no one picks up. Then finally I get through, explain myself to an English-speaking receptionist, who puts me on hold while I am transferred to another officer who doesn't speak English. Each time I must explain 'the situation' I feel like I am being punched in the face. Like a boxer, I prepare myself for each blow. Yet when it comes, I'm shocked.

I finally reach Cristina. 'Okay,' she says, 'you want a copy of the investigation?'

'Please,' I say, 'yes.'

'Call back on Monday,' she says. 'I have a lot of work today.'

So that's that. I cross my fingers and set an alarm for Monday, as if I'll forget. My heart begins to settle down, the tension in my gut relaxes and I feel wetness between my legs; the gentle slipperiness of hot blood.

I have told the story of me in Lisbon at eighteen being attacked by two young men hundreds of times. The more I simplified the story, the more comfortable with it I became. I integrated the facts of it into my identity. I had been terrified, but I wasn't harmed, not beyond repair. While afterwards I trusted people a little less, I didn't fear sex, or men, or even travelling alone. And I didn't think about the word *trauma* until years later, when I noticed that my nerves could not hold still, not in even a minor crisis.

On the way to a brother's twenty-first birthday, my family, all packed into the butter-beige '80s Volvo, ran into a cyclist. The cyclist was at fault, and no one had been going fast enough for the accident to have caused injury. But the guy hit the bonnet of the car, and automatically I screamed 'Oh-my-god-oh-my-god-oh-my-god', tears bursting out of me. Mum shouted at me to calm down while she pulled out her crisis-management package (*How do you feel, don't get up, an ambulance is on its way*) and Dad screamed at him, 'Jesus wept! Whaddayou think you're doing?' and the cyclist said, 'Don't call an ambulance, please, I don't have insurance.' And he was absolutely fine, although perhaps a bit of a bonehead, but it was too late for me, my night had been ruined, the fantasy that things are somehow safe, which you need to have if you are to do anything at all, had been pulled right out from under me.

There were other times: a little white dog we all thought had been killed at the traffic lights, but which popped out from under the bonnet a second later, unharmed. A kinky nothing said to me by a lover in bed, the same words that Salvator had said to me as he pinned down my wrists, urging his friend to violate me. A kitchen fire at a dinner party, where the thud of terror said *don't try to fight it—RUN,* to my embarrassment, while the friends I'd been dining with successfully smothered the fire with tea towels.

'This happened,' I used to say to friends, and therapists, 'and now here I am, exactly as you see me.'

11 February 2017

When I was a little girl, my favourite aunt said of me: she's been here before. She might have said this in response to the fact that at five I 'preferred soymilk', or that I opened packages with undue precision, or simply that I reminded her of herself—we share qualities, among them a love of beautiful objects that transcend context and time. But it's true, too, that I was a little girl who longed to be old, old, old—twenty, thirty-five, fifty, sixty-eight—because oldness was wisdom, age was elegance, grace was strength and power was freedom.

I didn't know that spring carries with it its own knowledge.

—You knew.

—She knew, but only in the inviolable way a person knows but does not understand.

12 February 2017

Yesterday, Dom and I walked through the yellow city. Dodging the street dealers who work the tiled plane of the Praça do Comércio, we crossed paths with a group of young people, clearly backpackers. An odd assortment of eighteen-year-olds—fat and thin, pimpled and pimped out—presumably having come together hastily at the hostel's breakfast bar that morning. Legally and morally, and maybe financially, they are adults, but the softness of their features betrays them.

> —'To know and not to understand is perhaps one definition of being a child.' (Claudia Rankine)

Cloaked in a sheepskin coat down to his knees, his tight curls shaved to a fade, their leader puffed on a cigarette while he walked. No smoker in their right mind smokes while they are walking. But a young smoker smokes not because they can't but smoke, but for the gravitas they believe smoking lends them.

> *—You remember someone telling your nineteen-year-old self, I'm surprised! I thought you were thirty.*

Thirty.

Jesus.

> *—You puffed your cigarette at them and beamed.*
>
> —Now and then, the uncrossable threshold.

—*A form of desperation, nostalgia. Speaking to the dead.*

—The dead are everywhere, like God.

The group passed us by, not noticing us. 'Watch out,' my ancient spirit urged them. 'Watch out for yourselves.'

13 February 2017

It's Monday.

So.

I dial the number.

Again.

A surge of adrenaline.

Detective Cristina Serinia: 'Okay I need a little more time. Please will you call back tomorrow?'

I hang up, exhausted. A bright acid curls inside my belly.

14 February 2017 (Valentine's Day)

Is aging the slow expenditure of a finite source of energy?

Some of the other resident artists are going out for a drink, and might we like to join them? There is no way we are going out. Dom and I heat up some dinner and crawl into bed.

We open the laptop to watch a dumb movie on Netflix. Because I'm writing about sex crimes and reading sad books by Svetlana Alexievich, Claudia Rankine and Peter Handke, I want a film to wash over me, to leave me feeling numb and easy.

> *—You don't even like movies.*

> —Books have more interiority. They are about insides as well as surfaces, not only surfaces.

But I do enjoy the passivity of watching films. So rarely do I feel so passive that I trust myself to be carried, without objection. I. I've seen them all.

> —All she asked for was a dumb movie to put her to sleep.

Well, we try.

Dead Calm (1989) opens with Sam Neill returning from his naval duty to find that his infant son has been killed in a car accident with his wife, Nicole Kidman, at the wheel. In the wake of the tragedy, the couple take an open sea yacht trip to reconnect. A dinghy containing Billy Zane, whose own ship is foundering, approaches the yacht; they let him on board. All of Billy Zane's boatmates have apparently died of botulism, which seems unlikely, so the couple lock him in the bedroom and Sam Neill leaves Nicole Kidman on the yacht to go investigate. In Billy Zane's sinking ship, Sam Neill discovers a bunch of dismembered, bare-breasted corpses. Sam Neill realises his rookie mistake and tries to paddle his way back to the yacht but, oh, too late. The ship has been commandeered by Billy Zane. Subtext: Nicole Kidman's imminent rape. Sub-subtext: the real victim of rape is the rape victim's husband.

We turn it off.

The premise of *Cape Fear* (1991) is that Robert De Niro, an ex-con, freshly out of prison for rape and battery, goes after

Nick Nolte, his former lawyer, for defending him improperly. The key ingredient is that Nick Nolte found evidence that the victim had been 'promiscuous', which is apparently a defence in a rape trial, but due to the severity of Robert De Niro's violence, Nick Nolte decided to withhold that 'evidence'. Nick Nolte is now compelled to protect his hot wife, Jessica Lange, and his prize, the sexy teenage daughter, Juliette Lewis, from imminent rape, while also suppressing his secret, which is that in his spare time, he plays very physical squash with his attractive younger colleague. To recap: a lawyer didn't appropriately slut-shame a rape victim, for which he feels real regret, and now the rapist, recently out of jail, is coming after the lawyer's women.

Nope, I say. No no no.

Indecent Proposal (1993) stars Robert Redford as a billionaire who would definitely touch the waitress's arse while she poured his wine. Demi Moore stars as a hot young out-of-work real-estate agent who is 'satisfied' because her husband, Woody Harrelson, is nice to her, and Woody Harrelson plays an aspiring architect who is also out of work but needs to finish building his dream house so that the world will recognise his extremely special talent. The couple go to Vegas to throw away their last five grand, which they do. Robert Redford, meanwhile, notices that he wants to shtup Demi Moore, and knows that, based on their difference in financial status, money will be an effective means of achieving this goal. Robert Redford coerces Demi Moore into gambling one million of his dollars at a very public dice table, a tell-tale sign of sociopathy, and then he thanks Woody Harrelson for lending out his wife so generously. In real life, everyone knows that pretty much anyone would sleep with anyone else for one million dollars, no questions asked. So the real question underpinning the tension is: what does Demi Moore value more highly—her husband's sexual ego, or her husband's creative aspirations?

'OFF!' I scream.

I open my Svetlana Alexievich book, *Zinky Boys*. One of her subjects, a private from the Grenadier Battalion, speaks of the first time he witnessed someone being shot:

> It's like a nightmare you watch from behind a sheet of glass. You wake up scared, and don't know why. The fact is, in order to experience the horror you have to remember it and get used to it.

15 February 2017

They say that eyewitnesses are unreliable. Stories are told of rape survivors who made sure to rigorously study their attacker's face during the assault for later identification. On this compelling evidence, innocent men are said to languish in jail until they are freed on the back of new DNA test results. Often this story is the story of a white victim and a black perpetrator, and it speaks to cross-racial blindness, or it speaks to structural racism and white women's complicity in it. Other times this story is about the memorisation act, about how every memory, once recalled, becomes a re-remembrance, a new memory made, mildly altered from an earlier version.

'Were they black?' The (white) police officer had asked me.

'No. White,' I said. White and rich.

I gave the detectives the scrap on which Tomas and Salvator had inscribed their email addresses.

'What were you wearing?'

Do they ask that question to victims of theft?

These were early social media days—hi5, something like that—and it wasn't as simple as jotting a name into a search engine. But, with the email addresses, Salvator's profile soon emerged, and with it, pictures of him surrounded by his friends. One picture, shot from below, showed a group of teens huddled in a circle.

> —That's him. With the big white mouth, celebrity teeth.

I sat in the back of a police car as we backtracked. 'Where did this happen?' an officer asked as we drove along the banks of the Tagus to its mouth, then along the beach. Then, a right. 'Around here?'

> —Feels right.

> —*Felt. Awful.*

And then a family of high-rise apartments with anonymous faces. 'Take your time,' the woman detective said to me. I took my time. But still, it was impossible to say with authority which apartment had been *the* apartment.

The detectives returned to the site with photos printed from Salvator's profile. Showed them round the neighbourhood. 'Do you know these men?' they asked. And then, a day or two later, I was called in to identify them.

I braced myself for the first of the two line-ups. Salvator was easy. Unusually handsome and unusually unperturbed by the situation. The sight of him filled me with rage. And fear.

—*Yes, you were afraid.*

Then, the Tomas line-up: I knew who it was I was supposed to be identifying, the only one in the line of young men who vaguely resembled my memory of Tomas. But somehow, my memory of him, only a few days old, was totally altered. Amorphous in my imagination, he had become a composite of faces I already knew, erasing all of Tomas. But I saw in his face the look of fear, and identified it. Tomas was the dark-haired boy who looked like he had been crying.

—*Even* you *had been holding it together.*

—What entitled him to his tears?

I walked quickly from the dark ID closet into an open room that resembled a classroom—which I now remember, as if in a dream, as an actual classroom—dropped my head and sobbed. The male detective who had accompanied me throughout this allowed my tears for a moment, and then he said, 'You know, I've done this for a long time, and I've talked to those boys, and they're just dumb kids. They're not the monsters we usually deal with here.'

To this day, I have never met a monster.

—*You haven't?*

—Is she lucky for that?

16 February 2017

While waiting for the Skype call to go through to Cristina's office, I absent-mindedly write in my notebook:

> THIS IS MY STORY. YET I CANNOT FIND
> THE DOCUMENTS.
>
> THEY ARE MINE.

I'm navigating yet another obstacle separating me from attaining a simple slice of hot photocopied paper. That paper contains the information *I* need to move on. Move on: no. That's not right.

> —*Move on. Move along, please. Is what police officers say when the public is being public. Too emotional too curious too badly behaved.*

I mean. I am not an idiot. I understand that just because something happened to me doesn't mean that the suppressions of time and the failures of memory and the most human of all errors, bureaucratic filing systems, should somehow suspend themselves and consort to deliver me exactly what I'm looking for.

It does not escape me, either, that what I'm looking for doesn't exist. I want a copy of the investigation, which has been archived for ten years and is seemingly impossible to dredge up; I want to find out how Salvator and Tomas described the events in their words, if only to scoff at their lies; I want to know what judgement concluded the trial, if only to suffer through a not-guilty verdict. But none of this really matters. None of this pushes the factory reset button, or assists my interior life, except to make me remember things my body has buried.

—What happened to you, really?

A moment of consciousness is just a fraction of time.

—It is all, a moment, you have.

But its material is made of every fraction that came before it, and its presence will predict the substance of all future fractions.

When I was a uni student, years ago, I edited the student newspaper. That kind of job unsurprisingly attracts meetings with all kinds of fringe types. Once, a middle-aged woman wearing loose denim came in, sat on the couch across from me, and said, coyly: 'I have a story. It's big.'

'Oh? What is it?'

'The government,' she said, 'NASA, the AFL, Iraq. It's all connected. And I have the evidence to prove it.'

It was difficult, I remember, to get her out of the office without causing offence. With each gentle dismissal, she heard an encouragement. When finally the woman left, she promised to send us her evidence, which she said was kept in a storage unit somewhere secret. Evidence that *it's all connected*. She went away and we never heard from her again.

—It is all connected, though. Truly.

When we say that a narrative is, or is not, someone's 'story to tell', what we unwittingly suggest is that when the story is *yours*, as in, it happened within time as you directly experience it, you are given some power over it. Is this the biggest betrayal of pop psychology via talk therapy? That in language a person can find sufficient tools to erect a life undisturbed by demons? Or the thought, even, that a person can comprehend what it is they have lived through.

> —Survivors of all things, always trying to reconstruct the moment they survived through.

> —*Strange, though, that even as you narrate it, you get to the horror point, and you think, this time, it'll go differently. But the film reel keeps playing through, all the way, and, whoosh: powerless.*

Tomorrow, I am taking a train out to the suburban court where my file is archived. I think. It's hard to say, really. I'll either get the copies I need, or I won't.

17 February 2017

Dom and I go on a trip out to the court where my 'process' file has been archived. The regional train races past the docklands beneath the red bridge, out towards the beach. To the left, the Atlantic Ocean opens up before me, slick and chilly. To the right, blonde apartments emerge in rows from the dense green hills strewn with wild yellow flowers. It was in there, in one of those apartments, that it happened. Inside them, I can tell you, there are marble counters and gold-coloured curtain rails.

When we find it, the courthouse is stark, fascist, latin-white. Paint curling off it. Inside, the wood panelling radiates under the sunlight. I give the young receptionist, who is wearing a small silver engagement ring, my notebook, where I have written my list of demands in Google-translate Portuguese.

> —*By now, you expect little.*

She calls over an older woman with plump cheeks who can speak English. 'You must apply to see the process file,' she says. 'It has already been archived.'

'I know,' I say. 'That's why I'm here.'

'What is your reason?' she says. 'Why do you want to see it?'

>—*You must have a reason.*

>—She doesn't say: to write an essay.

>—*They'll think* journalist. *They'll say no.*

>—(Truths like that can keep you from the truth.)

'I had to leave Portugal,' I say. 'I never found out what happened.'

>—*Is that why you're here, really?*

The woman looks at the computer screen and types. Finally she says, 'I can't tell you the sentence, but I can say the man, the accused, his sentence was annulled.'

'Oh,' I say.

'You will need to fill out a form to find the *sentença*, the precise judgement,' she says.

'Yes,' I say.

'The court will telephone once the judge has decided whether you can see the file.'

'Okay,' I say. 'I'll be in Lisbon another ten days or so.'

I take my vending-machine Diet Coke outside and smoke a cigarette in slow motion on the edge of a fence. Dom touches me sweetly and says comforting things that I can't hear.

There is a reason a person might not seek such a verdict for eleven years.

—'...willing suspension of disbelief for the moment...' (Samuel Taylor Coleridge)

'I guess it would have been unusual if they had been convicted,' I say to Dom.

—*Breathe in, the dusky smoke hits your lungs.*

'I mean. Evidence-wise—

—Injustice.

'There was nothing to prove whatever they did they did without my consent. So...

—*You're rambling...*

'They lied and they won. Liars win, violence wins. That's what is always being proven.'

—*Stop.*

—The two of them are not far from the beach. Twelve million people, plus however many untold millions more, were stolen and smuggled, across that water. So many drowned. Just a blink of an eye ago, and with the full permission of the law. Horror. The law is horror.

—*Those sparkling beaches tell you all you need to know.*

21 February 2017

Thing is, there *had been* evidence. But I guess it went missing.

After Tomas let me out of the room and out the door of the apartment into the hallway, I looked along the rows of identical doors and was struck with dysphoria. 'Where the hell am I?' I screamed.

'I'll take you,' he said.

He led me into the elevator, where we stood shoulder-to-shoulder, shaking with adrenaline. Then out of the lobby and towards his little car. 'Get in,' he said. So I did. A few hundred metres down the road, he pulled over, hit his hands hard against the wheel. 'Shit,' he yelled. 'I'm out of petrol.'

> —*You looked ahead. There was a petrol station within the field of vision.*

I thought: he's going to lock me in and rape me here.

> —*Nice plan!*

> —When recollecting this scene later, she noticed there was no one around. Not a soul. It was Sunday morning. The petrol station clearly wasn't open.

I swung the car door open and bolted down the hill. Tomas cried out after me but I didn't look back, not for minutes. Round corners and through bushy enclaves. I didn't slow down till I was down by the beach.

All I have to do is walk along here for like, ten kays, and I'll be home, I thought. I had about five euros on me and no bank cards. A car pulled up beside me.

'Where are you going?' asked the driver, an adult man.

I looked at him sideways, and thought: I am exactly the final girl in *The Texas Chainsaw Massacre*.

     —Hell or high water, you will survive this.

'I'm not going to hurt you,' he said. 'Look, I'm going into Lisbon. I'll drive you.'

No way, I thought. But also: just try raping me—I'll happily roll out of a moving vehicle! So I got in, scanned the door-handle-seat-belt situation for my impending escape. No central locking. Good.

'What happened to you?' he asked me. I told him. And burst, again, into tears. As I choked on my saliva, the man began kneading my thigh. First the knee, then higher, and higher.

'Don't touch me,' I hissed. And he looked at me as though I was nuts. As in: calm down, baby. I'm just kneading your thigh. Relax, relax. Relax.

He scoffed and gave me his hankie. We did not speak for the rest of the trip. When he pulled up by my hostel, the man pulled down the sun visor and it read: *Polícia*.

'Oh.'

'I'm a police officer,' the man said.

'I see.'

'There's a station just up the road. Go to sleep for a few hours, then go there and tell them what you told me.'

When I gave the tourist police my statement a few hours later, chipper and responsible as could be, I included the part about the police officer who drove me home. Not the part about him kneading my thigh. Just that he got me home, that I had told him what had happened, that he had pointed out the police station to me. I waited as they put out a call to all the officers who'd been on duty that morning.

None of them, apparently, had picked up a girl.

'But he did.'

'I'm sorry.'

    —*He did.*

When other people lie they make you look like a liar.

22 February 2017

There's this video going round where a beautiful female author and a man who raped her, many years ago, stand together on stage and talk to the audience about big ideas like accountability and trauma and forgiveness.

'A few years ago,' the woman—the rape survivor—says, 'it became apparent that in order to move on in life, I'd need to forgive this guy.'

'And when she made that decision,' the guy says, 'she passed responsibility for the crime over to *me,* the perpetrator.'

Everybody is sharing this video.

    —*It was already on you, though. All over you.*

The thing people like about this video is: here is another way to conceptualise rape.

—Okay. You get it.

The other thing about this video is: the institution that gives primacy to forgiveness—a primitive sort of Christianity—is the same institution that shames women into submission. Like: the meek do not inherit the earth. Anything that sells the meek short in this way is really just a tool of enslavement.

> —We have forgiven enough.

> —'If you take away my life, I'll give you blood to drink.' (The last words of Sarah Good, who was murdered in the Salem witch trials.)

In my early twenties it seemed as if all my female friends were in therapy, talking to an empty chair, addressing their mothers. Letters were written. Redemption was sought. The rationale was that it would be possible for these young women to 'move on' or develop 'healthy' relationships or 'love themselves' only when they forgave their mothers, who hated them.

> —Forgiveness is the wrong aim. Acceptance, even, too humble.

> *—Find, in those betrayals, the strength to exist.*

Around that time, I was grey area'd by an older writer. That grey area, somewhere between boldness and shame, knowledge and horror.

> —The field of sexual exploitation we feminists are not entirely supposed to admit exists, but which every woman on earth knows exists.

> *—Find, in those betrayals, rage.*

A few weeks after this troubling (for me) encounter, the writer gave a public talk. I didn't want to speak with them ever again, nor was I curious about the subject of the lecture. But I needed them to see me, just once more. Before they began their speech, they looked up and we locked eyes. I was slouched over a chair in the centre of the auditorium. My face betrayed no warmth, no familiarity, not a thing. They shifted their focus to their notes and did not look at me again.

—Look at me again and I'll kill you.

—*I'll give you blood to drink.*

23 February 2017

The courthouse has become my body's focal point of tension, I notice; I can feel my bones, every organ in my trunk, as we sit the train ride out. I can't focus on the pages of my book, so I look out the window. Brilliant light. The yellow of the flowers is violent.

This is the last time. The last trip I am taking out to the court. I received the email yesterday afternoon:

Venho informar que poderá proceder ao levantamento das cópias solicitadas.

[I hereby inform you that you may collect the requested copies.]

—Exactly what she wanted. This whole time.

The walk between station and courthouse is quick. Dom tries holding my hand; I don't know how to say *please don't touch me* without saying 'Don't touch me!', so I hold my arms close to me and hope he reads the gesture.

The court's archivist, João, is a gentle man. He smooths his hand across the open pages of the two thick binders, talking me through everything that happened after I left.

Salvator corroborated my testimony. He was not charged. Tomas was prosecuted. He was given a suspended sentence of twelve months, and was required to pay five hundred euros to a victim support organisation. Tomas then appealed the sentence, and his sentence was annulled.

As João methodically copies the documents, I swing to Dom. 'But Salvator was the evil one,' I say. '*Salvator*. Not Tomas.'

And of course I know in an instant that my memory was all wrong. I must have, at some point over the years, switched the names of the faces. And if I had been so certain about something so wrong, what else? What else had I changed?

> —Another day, another anxious train ride home. But this time the anxiety had an object.

We stop for Chinese on the way home.

The horror, horror, horror.

> Fried rice.

I have their full names now.

> Two Tsingtaos.

I am going to google the shit out of them.

> Garlic stir-fried greens.

Back home again, I search online.

—*Useless. Nothing.*

—A lot of people with names just like theirs. Even with their middle names, nothing.

Tomas must have changed his name. For sure.

—*Coward.*

I think about hiring a private detective.

I find one Tomas da Silva on Facebook, private account, and I message him.

Do you know me.

Blueberries

I was in America at a very expensive writers' workshop, maybe not expensive compared to say an MFA in America, but expensive enough that you'd have to save for a while to go, or else have someone pay your way, which I did, which was for the purpose of furthering my career as a writer-scholar under the auspices of a PhD in English at a university in Australia.

I was in America at a very expensive writers' workshop and I met a new soul friend, a woman whom I bonded with so intensely that by the end she told me that now she knew for sure that she wasn't a dyke, and by the end I knew I still had it in me to love women like that, but in this case I turned it off, because it was something else, it was an innocent line of understanding between us.

I was in America at a very expensive writers' workshop with my new-found soul friend, complaining that our very expensive faculty was somewhat mediocre—not the faculty member I was studying directly under, more specifically two of the very expensive male faculty who didn't prepare lectures and just ad-libbed at the almost all female, almost all forking-out-money-they-didn't-have students, who stared blindly and adoringly into the giddy promise that a two-thousand-dollar ticket offers on you.

I was in America at a very expensive liberal arts college, sitting on my rubber prison-issue mattress, trying to punch words on my two-hundred-dollar laptop that would turn 'I went to a very expensive writers' workshop and it wasn't perfect' into a salient political argument about the friction of class and gender and race against the surface of art in real-world institutions, and I was eating blueberries and I was naked but for my black silk robe, and I was disappointed not for the first time that 'excellence' was turning out to be mediocrity dressed up in money and maybe masculinity too, not the masculinity that is visible to us, brawny and street-smart, but *real* masculinity, which is reedy and tepid and well read and invisible.

I was sitting in a very expensive American college chapel, locked in the centre of a pew by bodies sitting at either end, listening to one reedy and tepid and well-read faculty member tell us that he'd considered reading us a lecture, which was also the introduction to his most recent book, but instead he'd decided to just stage a *chat* with us about general nonfiction concepts, and in doing so revealed that his sister no longer speaks to him because of the way he figured her in his books, and he can't for the life of him understand why, but that they are still in touch for the sake of his daughter, who—he reminded us several times—suffers from a 'weight problem'. The faculty member with the mute sister and the fat daughter later ended up embroiled in a workshop scandal, which saw the only woman of colour present abandon the classroom, and the only woman over the age of forty—a school teacher in her other life, apparently—take him aside to explain to him what he'd done wrong, for which he scolded her, the boom of it ricocheting down the corridor into the other very expensive workshops. He had simply critiqued a young woman's writing against the clothing she was wearing, and couldn't for the life of him understand why this had been so badly received.

I was in America, sleeping at the kind of very expensive liberal arts college that is so progressive it has gender-neutral toilets in some of its buildings, which is good, and necessary, a hard-won victory for all, though I choke at the thought of admiring a university that confuses charging its students eighty thousand dollars a year with radical acts, by which I mean what is the significance of gender-neutral toilets within an institution whose barriers to entry are configured so that, for example, a new migrant with modesty obligations as part of their religious convictions could or would never earn a degree within its walls, which is not to say that a new migrant with certain convictions would oppose the existence of a gender-neutral toilet but rather that it is something which cannot be tested or even really considered, because the unofficial motto codifying the morality of this college is 'communism, atheism, free love', all of which are sentiments I can get behind except for when these sentiments are possibly actually celebrating individuals wealthy enough to be free from class, free from community and free from the need to develop lasting bonds of mutual obligation, all because these individuals have benefitted from some radiant power whose axis remains mysterious to them. I was worried, at this very expensive writers' workshop, that the wool so to speak had been pulled over our eyes, that we had been stooged, that what we had been made to believe was most pressing was simply that which we could most readily and tokenistically address, *i.e. accommodating wealthy queers into mainstream wealthy spaces*, and I suspect that *this* is what is meant by hegemony, rule through the consent of the ruled, the distraction from material problems that are categorical and unsolvable by championing 'issues' that can be solved today by changing a sign on the door, issues that serve to empower individuals within a cloistered class environment rather than upend the economic inequity that is the foundation of institutions like it and, who knows, maybe they're the same thing but probably they're not. Hegemony is always at some level coercion, it is trickery, and the problem of this expensive college is not that it is a transphobic institution per se—though there is no doubt that it is—but that it naturalises an elite class into the logic of its own superiority and the violence of this could only ever be remedied by burning this institution to the ground and who in their right mind would do such a thing.

...

There were five minutes in which to pee during the break in a very expensive writers' workshop session and so with fifty women in the halls lined up for the stalls, I entered the male toilets— black and white tiles, Edwardian brass taps—and as I left the cubicle the reedy, well-read male faculty member walked in and he was shocked, he was really astonished to see me exit a cubicle in the so-called male toilets, and *really?* This is of course one of the many reasons why we need gender-neutral toilets; one of the many reasons being that same-sex spaces seem to produce uncomfortable and sinister interactions. When I was a young woman in the Women's Room at uni I freaked out a lot that I was a fraudulent feminist because I wore lipstick and I lived with my boyfriend, who was religious, and I didn't feel that the state-ment 'women aren't safe anywhere but here' was factual because in some ways I didn't feel safe in the moral judgement of that space, and I identified more with my boyfriend even though he believed in structures I couldn't see, ones spelled out in ancient texts, than I identified with these women with sturdy egos and chunky shoes, because he and I both lived in invisible places and we both worked shitty jobs for unpleasant people and we neither of us felt particularly entitled to anything much, but that was when I really believed in what you'd call *class difference*, and now I think perhaps that race and gender produce different class affects, and they produce variation in the ways that people learn to speak for themselves, and I understand better now that although I have no money, I *am* thinking about the *toilets* at a very expensive liberal arts college and this stands in for something, it stands in for a kind of class mobility that I have because maybe my race is my class now, or my class is the class of my peers, and part of me is proud to say that some of my friends now are borderline famous.

I was naked but for my black silk robe, wondering why it was that when I was eighteen I became the first person in my family to go overseas for anything other than economic migration and that this was it now, me *making it*, eating blueberries at an expensive liberal arts college complaining about expensive mediocrity which I didn't even pay for, waiting till it would be time for the sun to fade over the outdoor amphitheatre with a pond behind it where ducks would mate violently, and we'd all chuckle at that and strain harder to hear authors tell us stories that were not mediocre but not brilliant either because brilliance isn't what it's cracked up to be, just stories by storytellers, just storytellers shooting tendrils of words like silk at us, which we'd plant in our ears—the possibility of new constellations.

I was walking around moderately priced south-eastern Portland with my new-found soul friend, sweating and attempting to determine whether the rock-dog knuckleheads wearing AC/DC shirts on the streets were in fact real knuckleheads or if maybe they were ironic knuckleheads, which would make them more genuinely knuckleheaded, and this made me feel indignant and critical and cool yet also aware that a person could look at me and my sweat, my greasy hair and my dirty Nike Frees and think something similar about me too.

I was walking around moderately priced south-eastern Portland with my new-found soul friend, talking about writing and aspiration and how complicated these things were, like how do you live outside capitalism and still have dirty Nike Frees. We talked about the impossible, egotistical nature of feeling called upon to spend every day, each moment, give or take, writing, and the times not writing, either talking about writing or suppressing the urge to write in order to pay the dues of living in the real world, but also that conversely no one cares to give their permission for you to write, because it is a luxury of the gods, so you end up with this feeling like *it's so hard*, and *I'm so marginal* because in spending your time writing you offer very little to capitalism or, frankly, your community, yet on the back of your unpaid labour, festival organisers, publishers, printers, distributors and academics earn middle-class salaries. An idea I have is that arts professionals could tithe ten per cent of their incomes to pay the artists whose labour affords them their jobs, but this is an aggressive stance because there are other benefits to the role of the writer, benefits like authorship and hypothetical interestingness and sexiness too, particularly (or solely) for the young.

Before I was in America at a very expensive writers' workshop, a person asked me the question 'how did you become a writer', which I wasn't sure I was, and the story as it plays out in my mind is that I became a writer (if that was what it was) when I started to realise that I wasn't loved and that maybe I never would be: I was nineteen and poetry was snaking out of me because I felt badly treated, or I was newly aware that I'd colluded in my self-annihilation and the love I had sought out up until then was shit. I became a writer when I learned that I was a person and not just a figure inside another person's libidinal imagination—

I am still not entirely that, though, a person; still part of my brain is lobotomised by the fantasy of glory and worthiness in libidinal abjection and I have to somehow live with that. But that wasn't how I responded to the question. Instead I said something about failing to be good at university and failing to write decent American short stories and contemporary poetry and metred poetry too but still feeling compelled to have my new-found being seen: dancing was off the cards, wrong body, and music was my mother's trade, and acting made me nervous about lying, and painting was expensive. And so writing was like a triumph of being, it was the first claim I made on living outside someone else's love or not-love, approval or contempt, and at the same time it was a culmination of a failure of all other things. And this was not exactly the right answer or true, but it was not a lie, either.

I was wrapped in my black silk robe sucking blueberry juice from my fingers, relishing the colour of it inky and regal, pure decadence, because where I live blueberries are strictly a seasonal treat, but in the Pacific Northwest they're normal priced and abundant. The college food at this very expensive writers' workshop was locally sourced and organic, which you certainly can't argue with, but which brings up in me confused feelings about how morality is understood in places like this very expensive liberal arts college, as an innocuous topic but a cruel one, useful for slinging indictments across dinner-party tables, dinner parties at which the worst thing that could happen is that somebody might assume a passive-aggressive tone and another might fiddle silently in their discomfort. This dynamic is very common in the place I live, in places where your moral character extends from your decision to shop either at the shoddy little independent grocer, where the capsicums are wrinkled and shelves are half empty, or across the street at the organic grocer, where ten dollars will get you a packet of black teabags and little else. These scenes of dinner-table righteousness can only occur where the wars are buried deep underground, where the morality is decided, it's so over, because there's no situation left to test it against, no one who will scream let alone kill for anything more trifling than a pub brawl or a hatred of women, and the only way to be good here is to eat seasonally and organically, but still sometimes I shop at the independent grocer with the wrinkled capsicums out of a confused sense of class loyalty, and to make up for it I grow my own food a little and badly, and I scatter these pea-green snail pellets because I fear for the saplings, and the pellets are of course poison, I am poisoning the soil, and in my culture, this niche, comfortable and rather unpleasant culture, this sort of implies I am a bad person and I don't consider myself that, not really, but I am a person trapped inside a matrix of bad ideas bad histories bad reactions. Bad spirits trapped under my house back home move through the pine floors at night and I am sure the dread they impress on me is the hymn of a pellet-poisoned earth.

I was wrapped in my black silk robe pushing velvet blueberry skin against the roof of my mouth, a fleshy eruption, thinking about what it might mean to reintroduce shame into my culture, a thought experiment based on a conversation I had with a friend who is a judge's assistant and like me formerly a Catholic, about some of the things they'd forgotten to include in the law regarding women's safety, for example in my state it's not illegal to trick someone into having unprotected sex by providing false documentation of blood-test results and it's not illegal to start the sex consensually with a condom and then remove the barrier sneakily and ejaculate inside the woman, and this seems not only humiliating but dangerous, and yet the only thing you can really do about it is tell your mates and maybe if you're a bit aggro have a male friend go round to their house with a cricket bat, but basically you're on your own and imagine if you had a weapon called shame in your arsenal. But shame is useless these days, we only feel it about weight gain or having poor parents or being bullied at school, it's the wrong way around. What if shame, I thought, if shame was available to leverage against the selfish the dangerous the racist the gross, and this reminded me of the propriety involved with the organic-food moralism, which, while it may in fact be correct, as in, organic food is possibly better for the environment, it seems to be more about the entitlement of an elite class to impose its moral directives on the people whose labour allows them to be elite in some way or another, just as the moral temperament of the Victorians justified their aggressive economic expansion, their commitment to religious and moral regulations serving as a tool of dominance. And this is not quite the same, but it is often the people for whom power is not a birthright who consume decadently in public and I'm not talking organic-blueberries decadent I'm talking high-school girls in Juicy Couture I'm talking fine dining on a teacher's salary I'm talking health spas in Bali on a builder's salary, which we're supposed to tut-tut even if we're not the elite, because people who have *bad taste* in things are extravagant, are not supposed to have the money, and they're not supposed to be wasteful like the true elites who eat organic blueberries. And these food politics being the site of moral rigour in a scene in which it's basically legal to non-consensually ejaculate inside a woman invokes a desire in me to bring back Victorian repression but in the inverse—meaning bring back shame and maybe even honour, but the shame in this instance will be imposed upon the aggressive expansionists, on the church and the institutions that possess that authority now, and concede that the moral fortitude belongs to the people whose labour creates the organic-blueberry wealth. I know it's unpopular now, even, especially, on the left, where I situate my thinking, but I am somewhat concerned that God is nowhere anymore—and, well, it's religion's fault, it shamed the wrong acts—because this aggressive accumulation now simply justifies itself.

I was wrapped in my black silk robe sucking blueberry juice from my teeth at a very expensive liberal arts college when I read an interview with a friend of a friend, a writer who said that he always knew he was a writer, and I thought, *bullshit*, that only means he always knew he was an 'I', he was never a girl who imagined herself only in relation to, an object of the writer. Growing up I thought I would be an artist, as in a painter like my grandparents were, but really it was Grandpa who was the artist and Grandma was a glass-cutter an illustrator a drawer a teacher, it was she who did the housework and it was she who went to work when there was no money coming in. And to me, then, being an artist meant some weird conjugation of maker and muse, lover and wife, intellectual and subordinate, living wrapped in a black silk robe. I had a friend in high school who, like me, loved drawing singing acting reading, and we talked a lot about one day maybe becoming someone's muse, like, we were always ironic about it, *ha-ha*, but there was a touch of the Simone d. B. syndrome about it too: the only way we could imagine being something was attaching ourselves to its author, a living person in a male skin. We were pretty enough and precocious enough that boys wanted to get with us, so that's what we thought the route was (no pun); the goal I think was to get higher status guys in the cultural sense to want to fuck us, and that that would be some act of creation. But no, it's not. It's not. This friend's mum worked as a curator so when we were sixteen-seventeen we'd get to go to openings that were so extravagant and high class, and we'd wear luscious op-shop outfits and cheap-as heels and men would comment on how pretty we looked and we were able to think right then: *this* is *access*, *this* is the *beginning* of *making it*, even though those guys were just her mum's colleagues being mildly inappropriate and if there was anyone we'd actually want to get with it was one of the uni student casual workers behind the bar. And so at these events, these openings, I never once thought my name could be on the wall one day, though I was aware I could if I played my cards right end up like my peers, naked on the wall, represented by somebody else, so instead I'd just look to the immaculately dressed women who always introduced the artist and I'd think: *there* is an *important woman*. She's wealthy, she's charismatic, and it looks like she's at the centre of power. But she's not, or not entirely, she's just got a nice suit and a rich family maybe, and when she's dead in most cases no one will remember that she was ever alive. Then one day me and my friend were at a big gallery and I looked at a wall of photographs of famous European artists, artists whose faces you'd recognise as those of famous European artists, and for some reason I saw it all at once laid out and the only thing I could say was 'Where are all the women artists', like I had only just noticed, which could as easily have been where are all the Aboriginal artists where are all the trans artists where are all the Asian artists, except that we're talking about a group that constitutes fifty per cent of any otherwise marginalised population and any privileged one too. My friend laughed at me, but I could see that she knew it too, and we had both been raised by women who made art of various kinds but hadn't made big enough splashes to be up on that wall, and after that it became a line I said all the time—*where are all the women*—and this appeared *hostile*, maybe *obnoxious*, like I had been a feminist all my life but until then I hadn't always been complaining. Maybe it didn't happen just like that. But I remember the heat in my cheeks when at once I knew I couldn't laugh anymore about women's abjection. The normal woman who is just an object and the muse is the signifier's mistress. The feminist woman is the signifier's ex-girlfriend who he tells everyone 'has got a bit stalk-y'.

I was in America at a very expensive writers' workshop, trapped in the middle of a pew listening to a pale man riffing when I thought—I don't know if it happened like this but maybe it did—I thought, I don't want to be a feminist anymore because *I'm sick of complaining.* I'm sick of sitting through lectures like this and subliminally counting the number of female thinkers who are referenced, or not, thinkers from the colonies, thinkers who didn't do their thinking just because they were given the freedom to, were expected to. I thought: it's *humiliating*, I'm sick of interacting with reedy tepid well-read men and I'm sick of writing from behind the injury of colluding in my own oppression and not saying anything new because all I want to say has been said by other women and better.

I was at a very expensive writers' workshop and a faculty member, a mid-career writer of American fiction, gave a lecture about how she had only recently understood that she'd been pandering to the white male authority reader this whole time and now she was finally committed to changing her tune, and, well, I skipped this lecture, because the description seemed rudimentary to me, and instead I walked deep into south-eastern Portland with my new-found soul friend till we found a park filled with towering pines, majestic structures in the cathedral of the sky, breathing and groaning and creaking in slow motion, and for one moment I felt lifted, truly outside myself, and on the way back my soul friend and I sat down for a beer. By the time we returned to campus the women writers, a demographic which of course constituted ninety per cent of the cohort, and most of them white, were energised, really excited, because for perhaps the first time they'd heard a woman angry in her own words within the walls of a hallowed institution and I can't, I could never, begrudge a woman coming to consciousness, but it stung a little to witness it in 2015, and even now, these fist-bumping women, these new recruits to the *écriture féminine*, might not pick up a bell hooks book any time soon but maybe that's okay. I am an advocate of course for women's writing, for women writing, for writing that declares its difference; gender is complicated, but it's also sometimes a means of articulating your specific needs, though the sex binary is perhaps less helpful for gender non-conforming people with needs and experiences outside of that particular ontology, and both of these arguments can co-exist and why shouldn't they? On the one hand it is important for gender to be considered in any understanding of a text's materiality but on the other is the singularity of an author whose classes and categories are movable they are inconsistent they are disobedient. So what good is it to be a woman except to resist the universal that denies us specificity (as does the category 'woman'), to occupy a position as a female person in solidarity with other women? This is something I talk about with a friend who is trans and femme, whose femininity has been violently denied to them by the public and continues to be, and so is an expert in femininity more so than I am because for them their claim on it is a claim to a recognition of their full humanity, and in this sense their femininity is politically significant in a way that mine which is naturalised and unquestioned is not. One day my friend was telling me about the breasts they longed for, and how at some point they'd have to decide the what and the how, what 'type' of visible, legible femininity they might stake a claim on, and they said—'the question is not how large should they be, but how many?'—and this for me confirmed the answer to the question of *what is a female person*. And what is a female voice. And what is the point of continuing the class of women. The point is always to be in resistance the point is to play the point is to be relentless in the desire to unmask callous reductions the point is to multiply breasts the point is to love what is different.

I was in America, pondering very expensively my discomfort in the ready adoption of feminism in academic contexts and online when life goes on as usual, and perhaps my discomfort is old-fashioned distrust of cheap signals, it is based on my understanding that these realms are purely discursive and it is difficult for me to understand the tension between material and symbolic realms, as I am certain they are sometimes the same, but other times they are not. And in lieu of shame and in lieu of a material crisis like war or madness to test these ideas, perhaps the struggle is contained in the signifier after all. But then what is the relationship between these things: of the pale male faculty member gratuitously unaware of himself; of gender-neutral toilets that are entirely necessary and likewise naturalise very expensive liberal arts colleges into supposedly radical discourses; of the chasm between a student and a faculty member, the labourer and the elite; of the woman writer at last throwing off her shackles and writing, singing, in the voice of a woman, of herself; and of the limits of this category, woman, which has for so long remained static for fear that its hasty stitching will be revealed, that no one ever knew in the first place what a woman was and until we did how would we ever be able to say 'this is what a woman needs'? The last battle of feminism is not how will mothers also work nor is it female presidents nor will it be the warm embrace of transwomen. The last battle of feminism will be fought when the category of woman won't need to hide its epistemological limits, when the category exhausts itself by a change in the weather, when being female will not involve degradation and it will not involve shame and it will not involve a woman writer waiting forty years before she garners the resolve to write what she longs to write.

...

I was in America, complaining very expensively about the lack of equality between the sexes in life, a power dynamic that is replicated in the relationship between art and capital, marginal and elite, which expressed itself through the student–faculty dynamics of this writers' workshop, and all the while I felt the thud of guilt knowing that someone, like, I don't know, my own mother, would have wrung her neck to have been given the opportunity to attend her art's version of the workshop I was at; and then, a crack of anger that we're all supposed to feel nothing but grateful when we are chosen to participate in these elite expensive rites, our little ant egos light up and we cough up money when they say we have been accepted into the MFA PhD masterclass.

I was in America at a very expensive writers' workshop, working on my social mobility.

I was in America at a very expensive writers' workshop, working on my writing by working on my cultural capital, which is an impolitic statement but no doubt a true one. The accumulation of cultural capital for the purpose of social mobility is a stone-cold fact of life and yet usually, in writing, in art and in the academies, it is shrouded by and passed under the guise of something else. Yet if this form of accretion underpins each facet of the production and industrialisation of art, why does it follow that we don't much talk about it let alone admit when we are in on it too? This labour, this acquisition of esteem, is only marginally secondary to the production of the art itself—sometimes you'll see it where there's cultural capital and no art at all, just a fake artist standing in where their work should be, but the artwork was the hustle itself and this is obviously rage-inducing and frivolous but there it is, more common than you'd think, or maybe just as common as you'd think. And anyone who denies that this hustle is almost as important to the art itself is admitting their failure to understand the central role of capital in art. But being aware of its operation and participating in it doesn't guarantee its successful acquisition.

I was in America at a very expensive writers' workshop, working on my social mobility, which was foolish, not because social mobility and cultural capital are useless pursuits, but because people who have already passed into the field of the elite tend not to attend these very expensive writers' workshops. That the students did not know this proves that they had not passed, may never pass, into the field of the elite. Which is also not to say there were no deep, thoughtful, stylish writers attending this very expensive writers' workshop, because elitism is not excellence it is barriers to entry.

My new-found soul friend at the very expensive writers' workshop now lives in New York City, which means I don't see her, which also means she works in comms for a start-up in order to live in an apartment and feed her dog. My new-found soul friend is toying with throwing in her paycheck to go back to just writing and I know she needs to, it's how she will be able to write what her body burns to write, but also there's no endgame, devotion and talent and well-connected friends doesn't necessarily change the situation because the situation is too closely connected to the truths that linger just behind slogans and conspiracy theories. Anne Boyer says that writing 'is the production of culture is I hate culture is the world of wealthy women and of men'. Like all this emotional work I just did, just dumping this essay into my two-hundred-dollar laptop, which made me feel insecure and mediocre but also 'good' as opposed to devastated because the act of typing stimulates some reward system in my brain, writing this essay was only ever about articulating how best to go about reproducing—without pay, with minimal pay—the cultural capital that is exchanged between wealthy women and men.

The Museum of Rape

1.0

On International Women's Day I buy a waist trainer on Amazon. Do I want to upgrade to Amazon Prime? No, I don't. This is the last time. The last impulse purchase. Checkout. I mentally apologise to a lot of consciousness-influencing figures. Sorry, Gayatri Spivak. Sorry, Queen Latifah.

An individual is not responsible for the corsets they buy in time. I mean, I probably won't even use it. I hate working out. Never stick to regimens, beauty or other.

2.0

A video of the last sixty-one seconds before cumming, him breathing into his phone, 'I love you I love you I love you' (18.1).

I watch it in the writers' studio at the artist colony, alone. My bowels are full and hot blood is ready to erupt from me so I don't touch myself, though I simulate touching myself in my mind. Like, wanking, video, simulation, imaginary wanking; several tiers removed from the flesh centre.

It is not quite morning-bright yet, the air still champagne coloured, and the yellow mimosa are really singing.

3.0

There is a guy on the internet who is cataloguing every false rape claim in history. I discovered this log while trying to find out if anyone had done the same for every rape (4.2). He writes,

> In 2015, singer-songwriter Chrissie Hynde claimed she was gang-raped at the age of 21, and caused outrage when she appeared to blame herself for the violation. I have to say I don't believe any of these claims, and I hope they are not true, especially the one by Chrissie Hynde, whom I've always liked.

and this tickles me, pink, red, raw, all over. Does he mean: 'I always liked Chrissie Hynde, hope she didn't get gang-raped'? Or, 'I always liked Chrissie Hynde, hope she didn't lie about it'? The answer to this is too bad to think about. I think *Probably nobody has ever loved this person.* And everything is worse than it was.

4.0

A long time ago I shared a yellow house with a couple. They became my parents, though we were more or less the same age. This dynamic is sure to get old, and it did, and afterwards they became, particularly my 'mother', my first official former friends.

Awful at the time, losing friends like that, to something mundane like, I don't know, immaturity. Now just a thing that got assimilated with all other things. Like a hot dry wind gently sanding the surface of my body.

I look like this. Smooth.

Ninety per cent of all human endeavours are said to fail, which seems like a low estimate.

4.1

They were going through *something* during the time we lived together, and what they were going through really put the body, for me, into perspective. His heart was fluttering, pain stabbing. At one point they thought, *A heart attack*. Midnight taxi to the hospital. And she, cold-sweat waking in the small hours to horror scenes playing endlessly in her mind's eye. In the daffodil daylight, she bleached every surface and organised the crockery in a way that made living impossible.

We fought without words. I moved away.

But still I think about that friend who I saw as a mother figure, or perhaps an older-sister figure, and I feel thankful.

Our fourth housemate, though. Beloved by all, truly, really died. My love for him is old and uncomplicated. Though there are always regrets (11.0).

4.2

She had this idea, my housemate-mother, to make a museum of rape. Well, she said. There are museums for every tragedy, every genocide. Why not the persistent all-encompassing mundane treachery of rape.

I really thought, before our friendship closed down, that we would make this happen (13.0). I would, I don't know, write the catalogue. Maybe interview survivors and activists, or go through archives to find the most typical and awful and compelling and also the most enlivening stories of girls and boys and women and men who had lived through or lost loved ones to it.

She would do the meetings. Her brilliance. Her backbone. My looking like a stunned fish whenever I am asked to answer for myself.

Possibly there is already a committee for this museum. I wouldn't know.

4.3
So I wait.

5.0
I was thinking of a word.

Burrow duct gap hole   narrow crevice
    canyon corner   cavity black hole
supernova portal man   hole shadow
    shadow shadow   cleft space nook
underside pharynx cave passage pit
    absence valley   opening fissure
parentheses anus valley abscess chamber
    depression blow   hole depth slit
valley favour forgiveness.   I can't feel
    the edges. From   the beginning. Without
recourse to the beginning.

5.1
Lacuna.

5.2
I know what it's like to fall into an abyss.

5.3
I thought. Maybe. I could be. I, a saint. It would explain. Feeling
of constant stirred up. And voices. But not God. Mine.

6.0
My first assignment for a bilingual nightlife/city-culture magazine I worked at briefly in Saigon was to interview a Parisian
Viet Kieu artist who lived in District Two. In his studio,
spacious and awash with sunlight, hung massive oil paintings.
Confident, expressive work, but not particularly original. Sentimental, maybe. The piece he was working on hung in the
most spacious of the studio's quarters: seven long panels strung
together, depicting a vivid colour-scape, a few figures, some
words, patterns. Midway through my questions, the artist urged
me to look at the work in silence. I sat and looked without focus at
the brushstrokes, affected a serious demeanour. A few minutes in,
I felt heavy in my head. Holding a hand to my face I let my eyes
well with warm liquid. The artist, arrogant in his silence, gazed at
me inscrutably.

I let out a quiet sob. And said, 'I'm in Saigon because my
friend died. He lived here.'

And he said, 'Sometimes sitting with the work evokes these
feelings.'

And then, more kindly, he said, 'What's your friend's name? I'll write it into the piece.'

I blinked. What was his name?

'Sam,' I said. 'His name was Sam.' (5.2)

6.1

But his name was Dan. Daniel Wright. Sam was the name of another dead man entirely. A dead man who had never lived in Saigon, and one whose tragedy hung heavier on others than it did on me.

And so now Dan's memory is inscribed in a French artist's work, under the name Sam.

Five years now. Don't read the emails.

7.0

I read so much I don't know where my ideas come from (5.2). Who is speaking when I hear what I hear. Is that how words become mine? Too many voices. Too much. A human being is not sufficiently evolved for the internet.

I remember, with total clarity, the line, the story, but never who spoke it.

Alcoholism, maybe (12.0).

7.1

The design of literature is not to split specifically me into a thousand pieces tenuously linked. This sounds crazy but I am speaking, right now, to you in quotations; I have lived in untold houses. I have kissed all of their surfaces.

The design of literature is not to sow false memories

that might twist up through my chambers creeping for light.
Lie. Light.

7.2

Some time, not so long ago, I dreamed that the city of London had
found a way of keeping its pigeons within the city's limits. There
would be no more migration to the south (London's pigeons, in
real life, mostly do not migrate). In the dream I thought, *What a
charitable gesture*. That London would keep its avian problem to
itself. But the conveyer of this information corrected me: 'They're
not protecting other cities from an avian *problem*. They're keeping
the birds from being snatched up by competing cities.'

These iconic pests were, in my dream, the strict property
of London.

When, yesterday, this story passed into my consciousness,
I tried to remember where it had come from. At first I thought it
had been an anecdote told by my friend Nadia, who often recalls
odd stories she has read in Russian newspapers. Such as: Amer-
icans don't have sufficient power in their homes to boil water
by means of electric kettle, so they use a stove. In some cases, a
microwave. Learning of the latter, the Australians responded
with jolly surprise.

8.0

What I am saying is that I understand the total collapse of struc-
tured memory.

I asked myself, what does it mean to anticipate the loss
of one's rational function (7.0, 7.1, 7.2). 'Dementophobia' is an
internet-science kind of answer, 'a fear of losing one's mind'.

Though the chaos I witness creeping in at the margins of my consciousness is not the symptom of a phobia. I don't fear. I comprehend, rather, the unity of the tangles and plaques, cell death, I comprehend tripping into the lacuna with my hands tied behind my back.

8.1

Tawhid is the Islamic concept of God's unity. It is one of the core concepts governing the faith.

If *everything* is (7.1, 8.2). Then a single human could never be King. For example.

The worst thing in the world is when an Anglophone drags another people's language into their burgeoning awareness of the limits of ontology. But I could have converted on the spot when I first studied this concept, *tawhid*. It described everything I felt to be true, the molten lava of everything knowable, but which I had never had a name for. And what has that got to do with a materially located method of worship.

8.2

Sudden knowledge that I, the puniest least consequential human being, am the same as the love feeling of looking at the ocean. The same as warm milk in a cow's udder. A perspex box full of pink plastic children's toys. A new knife set won in a raffle. The sound of someone's voice you have known since you were twelve. Garden pavers. A too-big starched prison uniform. A baby's first possum encounter. A drunk boy at the train station. An oyster's pearl. Saint Catherine of Bologna. Drones owned by the United States military. The idea of bowling. The stiff flake of skin in the middle of her bottom lip. The existence of fascism. A well-curated newsfeed. The delicate tops of carrots.

You.

9.0

Genesis exodus leviticus numbers deuteronomy kings one kings two corinthians one corinthians two ruth is how I remember it, wrongly. Although truly I thought I knew it by heart. My teacher, whose daughters were goths, insisted on my learning it. She played the cello, I think, which was charmingly the same shape as her body.

When I go back to witness the true order of the books, I find I am again reading the Song of Songs.

> *Your name is oil poured out.*

King Solomon, such a terrible patriarch. And yet.

I wanted to marry God (15.0).

10.0

The drummer from Silverchair, Ben Gillies, and his wife, Jackie, once sat next to me on a flight to Melbourne from Newcastle (16.0). They were relocating. So this was just before Jackie became a famous monster on *The Real Housewives of Melbourne*.

Ben ordered a tiny bottle of shiraz and a plastic box of crackers and cheddar, which I found tremendously lavish. I didn't have things like twelve dollars to waste at the time. Jackie asked me and I said. I'M A WRITER. Jackie said, 'My husband, Ben Gillies, is a famous musician.' Ben said, 'Jackie here is a famous psychic.'

'Cool,' I said. 'So, Jackie,' I asked. 'What do you think is in store for me?'

'You're going to be big,' she said.

I smiled coyly.

'You're going to be a very important music journalist.'

11.0

The feeling is devotion. (5.2, 8.2)

12.0

Alcoholics will tell you that if the first time you drank you blacked out, you are one of them.

The first time I fell down the stairs I felt nothing. Someone's older sister showered me, draped me in cool sheets so that I might live. One of my brothers told everyone I got my stomach pumped. But really the nurse just gave me charcoal to drink and said, 'Sleep it off.' Probably they had girls with real stomachs to be pumped. Everyone always overdoing it. He just needed a brush with danger to enhance his social status. That danger was me.

12.1

But I didn't choose hunger, hunger chose me.

But I didn't choose. Hunger, hunger chose me.

But I didn't. Choose, hunger hunger chose.

13.0

There will be problems inherent in the realisation of the International Museum of Rape.

13.1

Horrid. Rape, a stony, brutal word. The threat of the word possesses us: the way that we permit our legs to walk, throat boxes to talk, the way that we might place our arms at our sides as though it were natural to stand, or to possess a human body.

13.2

Ubiquitous. Like unity (8.1). Do you know? All human beings descend from one woman. The name given to her by scientists is Mitochondrial Eve. All our matrilineal lines converge in an unbroken chain to her. And early Homo sapiens commonly reproduced under rape's aegis. It is through the rape of our maternal ancestors that each of us exists.

One could say that rape precedes all other acts of violence. All other oppressions. Without it there are no human beings on earth on whom to inflict violence. No bodies to put to work no children to starve no workers to stab open the coal face to pour carbon into the shimmering sky. How could this fact be contained within a building, a mission statement, a human mind.

13.3

Fraught. Monumentalising this suffering seeks to, in some small way, honour lives, life. But the victims, the depth and breadth of cultural, legal and narrative modes for dealing with (or not) this violence, ought not be translated into a single tongue, the lingua franca of the museum. The museum, after all, has functioned to produce singular forms of cultural authority.

13.4, 13.5, 13.6

Who will pay for it. Where will it go. How can we live with this.

14.0

A mental-health website: 'The fear of losing one's mind is just a symptom of anxiety.'

Going Crazy = Anxiety?

> Anxiety can make you feel like you're about to lose your mind. It can be incredibly debilitating, and cause you to think that something terrible is happening to you. But it's often just caused by anxiety.

I suppose this is useful advice. In that it promotes a calm, rational approach.

My boyfriend's ex-girlfriend once spoke in Greek to him all night.

'I don't speak Greek,' he said to her.

'I know,' she said. 'That's why I'm speaking it.'

She was also thinking in Greek, she told him, in case he or anyone else thought they might try to read her thoughts.

My boyfriend's ex-girlfriend was scared of losing her mind.

She left him for Cyprus without saying goodbye.

But probably it's often just caused by anxiety.

15.0

At eleven I hungered for cloistered life (11.0). Longed for visions of the virgin. Thirsty candles. The smell

> of brass. Young knees violet
> with carpet burn. A sister's
> palm stroking my

back. 'My little cat,' she'd say
to me. While I tried to remember
the Beatitudes.

Blessèd are the poor meek mourn hunger merciful clean peace persecution.

Willed for the ghost to find me, strike my spine, shake me until I became alive (8.2, 12.1, 16.0).

But she never came.

At thirteen I took my magic elsewhere.

15.1

At twenty-eight I visited my patron saint. Catherine sits upright on a golden throne deep in the mediaeval bowels of Bologna. Stiff habit; her leather hand grips a ruby-encrusted crucifix. Patron saint of artists and temptations. Died 1463. Mysteriously mummified. Scientists can't explain it. At her burial site, so it goes, somebody smelled roses. The sweet odour of sanctity. 'We've got to get her out of there!' is what I imagine they said. 'Get her on that throne. And would someone *please* install some cherubs?'

Saint Catherine's face is like a rotten apple.

In the dark chamber before my patron saint, a woman sat on her knees. Weeping. Hushed magic spilling from her lips. I did not take a selfie.

16.0

I suppose my lover in Newcastle was like God. In that I wanted to marry him too. What a pity. I waited for his blood to raid me, thick and pulsing. Wanted to feel the shock of me. For a line to fall down round me as opposed to you, wife. Of. Flame. What a shame.

Unlike God, his hands were purple.

I didn't know about unity (7.0, 7.1, 8.1, 8.2, 11.0, 15.0).

17.0

After all my complaining about weddings in my life (and there has been complaining) I think this year I will have one. A bureaucrat's office in Denmark, nation of handicapped mermaids and express weddings. There is love with him, just like a row of teeth or an avian problem (7.2), and a visa too. But mainly there is life. Swampy, vivid life. And shaking it until the line is buzzing.

17.1

Quaker lovers crumble to their unblinking knees in silence. No priest. Stare it out.

The Liberation Tigers of Tamil Eelam would go off just the two of them and declare their new status. Word of mouth love amid terrible violence.

I don't like these things, which signify unity, to be mediated by the King.

18.0

The International Museum of Rape will be a solemn affair, like church, where I once mis-placed my reverence. Church, though, being its own museum of rape, will have to pay dearly.

18.1

The International Museum of Rape will be a large dome, an echo chamber, where the name of every woman in the entire world, and the name of each of her children and the children she could not would not have, will speak itself. It will be built of inexpensive material, collapsible, transportable to every carpark in the world. The sound will be tremendous. Every surface will be rippled with braille. Animals will be welcomed. And each space will be decorated by a furious arrangement of flora. Thousands of domes will pop up around the globe, maybe even one hundred thousand. And what will happen within these spheres is momentary chaos, is harmonious dignity.

Someone might call this a temple.

19.0

My friend Adam was a superior altar boy. Much better than giggling me. The nicest guy, perhaps, I've ever known. When we moved, he and my drama teacher were rumoured to be the only ones who missed me. He dated a glamorous girl with a rose tattoo on her breast who worked at the fruit shop. Like Carmen Miranda. Adam's father had killed himself. A boy teased him about that and my older brother punched him. My brother was punched in the face in return and has the black tooth still.

Sometimes the Father would give Adam a cigarette, or maybe Adam stole them.

When I remember Adam I feel touched as though a warm gas is spreading over me between the cells of my skin.

His name, though, might have been Sam.

19.1

Saint Catherine wrote the treatise *The Seven Spiritual Weapons*, a wild title for a wild book which, if written today, might provoke a schizophrenia diagnosis. But saints are like that.

She writes:

> *Whoever wishes to go up, let him rest not*
> > *From thoughts, from speaking works and doing deeds*
> > *And always exerting himself in God*
> > *but with discretion, so that when our adversary, like*
> *a wicked traitor, assails us from ambush, we can defend*
> *ourselves.*
> > *By 'from ambush' I mean, when under the appearance*
> *of good he wishes to kill you, for there is as much danger*
> *in too much as in too little.*

19.2

Catherine was one of those sisters who allegedly died a virgin. Which is to say, she was a sister.

Before I was born, Mum, another Catherine, worked at an old folks' home. She nursed a lot of ancient sisters as they died of cervical cancer. 'It's the most painful death,' she told me. 'Excruciating.' So I was happy to announce my first Gardasil shot, the vaccination against the sexually transmitted human papillomavirus, which is the cause of cervical cancer.

Mum was shocked. 'Maybe there's another way of getting cervical cancer,' she said. 'I mean, they were *sisters.*'

Maybe it's evidence that I'm from the time I am from, but I had always assumed that nuns lived in the nunnery as punishment for their passions.

19.3

But, you can see, Saint Catherine of Bologna knows that what possesses her is uncontainable (5.2).

Satellite

The librarian gestures towards a desk and chair by
the window, so I follow her hand and sit down, spread
out my books next to a young guy, seventeen maybe,
who is eating a meat pie. It's a quarter past ten in
the morning and he's eating a meat pie with sauce
from a brown paper bag, and he's reading a magazine
about sneakers, and for this sequence of facts alone
I adore him, but also I would like it if the pie funk
was not so intense. The window is partially obscured
by a council design, something to remind passers-by
that this is a diverse community in case they hadn't
noticed. I am sitting now with a stack of histories
of this small part of the world that I know best, but
don't really know, not really. When I was sixteen

they didn't have the desk at the library window, just an armchair or sometimes no furniture at all, so I'd sit on the floor with my backpack next to me in the sun, and I'd read about communism and existentialism and surrealism and dada, and I wore a beret, I think, and I saved my Macca's income to pay for a French tutor because we didn't have French at my school, and I knew I didn't have a real education because that was the index. More than a decade later I'm sitting here breathing in meat-pie steam but now I am reading about chain gangs and scarred trees and bodies buried deep beneath the tram tracks and I don't know French and I am horrified. I am trying to remain horrified lest this horror slips away, I am horrified by what started here two hundred years ago so that in the early 2000s I could dream about Europe propelled by junk-food money and mass-produced cliché hats made from the hair of an introduced species that has ravaged this land.

Now that I know I am parochial—and still I am embarrassed by this fact, by all the things I did not become—now that I know that the only constant in my life of elective insecurity is my proximity to a tram line, an artery thumping out north from the city, I am also certain I don't belong here, because I don't, but there's nowhere else to go but ashes and dust, or Scotland. And now that my parochial character is clear to me it's too late: my roots have dug in deep like those of the serrated tussock, which is an introduced grass species that thrives everywhere by choking its competitors, that avoids detection by passing for a native species, and this laboured metaphor is trying to say something about colonial figures like me who'd really like to not make things worse than they are, but who by simply accepting the yellow blotted sun through the pane of glass, by accepting the home built atop spirits silent and angry, have roots that are caught in the seams of rotten foundations. I know this fantasy will be demolished someday and the stories trapped beneath it will finally go free, but by then there'll be no one there to listen, and this sadness is worse than anything.

When we first moved here, my family thought the neighbours sophisticated and cosmopolitan because unlike us they had friends over at all hours, talking into the night, drinking sweet black coffee in the kitchen we could see into from our side window. Later we learned that this late-night banter, the visitors at all hours, was grief; their teenage son had been bashed to death barely a block away on Sussex Street by someone not even from our grim and frankly quite horrifying neighbourhood. My parents held us close but they couldn't always know where we were and with whom, and there was a lot of making friends with loner kids who lived there too, and tagging of abandoned factories and smoking Dunhills and then there was also romantic stuff happening, like once I gave my boyfriend a wristie in the underpass at the velodrome and just recently, just the other day, I drove out to the secluded carpark where instead of studying he and I used to park and fuck in his car in the black night under one yellow street lamp, and I sat, just the other day, in the car and I thought, how am I alive, how was I not dragged from that car and hurt right here, where the air smells like dirty oil-fried chicken because of Cammaroto Poultry on Charles Street and like burnt plastic because of Tontine Fibres on Bakers Road, and I was so in love with him, heavy, and I'm happy I suppose to be alive, but these things stick to you, they stick to you like burrs do in your socks.

These car nights took place in an empty lot next to one of the countless 'reserves' in the area, just patches of grass, dead spaces empty of promise, maybe one shrub or a grubby old grey box gum and some vintage-spec graf. At Sanger Reserve it said FUCK OFF OR TROUBLE and at Hosken Reserve it said LIVE RIDE WRITE ten metres tall, which was gloriously romantic, though I think in this context 'write' meant graf, and at a reserve without a name it said WATCH OUT FOR THE SUSSEX STREET BOYS signed off by Macca and Bluey. A council 'reserve'—nothing but light and grass—is a site reserved for something *else*, a site of potential, the potential to cancel out the damage of the garbage factories or the potential to make life more pleasant for the young taxi drivers who lived next door to us who shift-shared their beds because they were too many for their little unit. But to me the council reserves were unkept promises and unmet potential, and rubbing that in people's faces makes them want to cause trouble and bury their crimes in the knee-high patches of introduced grass species. These reserves are reserved for a time in the future when the council might dig up the soil to build spaces for deck chairs for residents in the future who deserve them, only to find the bodies, all the bodies, waiting to tell the stories that no one wants to hear.

I was living there around the time they converted Pentridge, Australia's most hellish prison, into medium-density apartments for the upwardly mobile. I search 'pentridge village where are the bodies' and discover that most of them, the prisoners who were murdered in that frightening place, by others or by the state, Ned Kelly, Ronald Ryan, have been exhumed and either returned to their families or left in the morgue awaiting identification, what a time to be alive. And, full circle, when the owners of Pentridge started selling off the D block as wine cell-ars *ha-ha* one of the inmates bought his old cell to store his Grange. I used to go running down Merri Creek to Coburg Lake, which skirts the edge of Pentridge, and it's the only place I can think of in Moreland where you can find a platypus that's not actually a misidentified rat, and when you're near the water you can for one second imagine what it might have been like, long grasses lizards birds, if John Batman had walked through this space and thought, maybe I'll just leave it as it is, maybe I'll just leave it to the people who know how to live here to live here and save everyone all the trouble. Because that's what it is, it's enshrined and systematic trouble that no one knows how to undo, because, apart from the one platypus who moved back to the area and maybe her one platypus friend, this trouble can't be undone.

But I am one of those people who is always baulking at injustice; I can't look at a rat without thinking about how sick humanity is. Had I been male, this might have been of use to some kind of extremist organisation, or to federal politics, but because I am female I am contemptuous of male power, and because of this my body is a body of emasculation, and because of this I just have a bad attitude. I dig my fingers into the earth in front of my house and I get it under my nails, weeding round the pearly succulents, because that's supposed to release serotonin and I wonder what on earth we are doing here, as in us, the rats, how are we all here now in this place, and I remember at high school a prized skill was being able to tell what *nasho* someone was by looking at them, and a lot of it was to do with how a person coded themselves fashion-wise, but it's true that some had a great knack for telling apart a Lebanese and an Iranian a Vietnamese and a Chinese an Eritrean and a Somali, and in the same place the white kids played up their Irish or whatever background because they didn't want to be left out of the fun, and you're not supposed to talk about things like this in adulthood because it's pretty offensive but I think that although *problematic* it was in earnest, acknowledging the dislocation each person felt in their heart and connecting somehow through its affirmation. And all you have to do with so many families, poor families that were altered irrevocably by industrialisation and imperialism, is scratch back a few generations and no one knows a thing, the line fades away to the primordial bodies moving around looking for food, for work, gravitating to places to nurture their young, protect them from nature's brutality, like the rat family and the warm underside of my fridge.

After travelling overseas when I was eighteen, my first attempt at leaving, I was in debt and so I moved back to the end of the tram line, back past the factories, back home. Mum and Dad were not as thrilled to have a grown adolescent living with them as I was to pay no rent and so I stayed away from the house a lot. One of the places I stayed away at was a warehouse where some friends and a boy I was dating casually were living, smack bang in the middle of Brunswick. They were wild people and truly bohemian, as in they didn't notice the squalor and thought my homework was endearing, and with them it was a different Brunswick from the underage gigs at the Town Hall and the tinnies in alleyways, but still Savers was a central theme along with the food bargains like Tiba's and Green Field. The main reason this guy I was dating casually was dating me casually was because he was not interested in me as a young woman in love, not really. So one night I went to a poetry reading with another boy, a serious young man from another city, good looking but not very funny, who was doing his masters at Melbourne 'for the pedigree', and from memory, it's not like I can ask him about it now, we drank boxed wine and argued about whether Sartre's communism was genuine (I stand by my no) and we made out in the taxi. His apartment was on the third floor and overlooked the warehouse of my friends but I didn't point it out. In the morning we awoke naked though we hadn't slept together, you know, screwed, but for whatever reason we just stayed naked all morning, and he made me coffee and he said, I'm glad we didn't sleep together last night, that would have been contrived, and I had no idea what that arrangement of words was supposed to mean but I stood there on the balcony, topless, maybe to seem sexy or adult, and I looked down along the piss alleyway and across it to the warehouse where some hippies I didn't know were moving terrible furniture and I gave him my assent, yes. Yes, that would have been contrived.

...

Before it was Coburg Coburg was called Pentridge, the satellite city built around the foul prison, the 'bluestone college', secure housing for the indentured labourers who built the road from Melbourne to Sydney, prisoner chain gangs carving the stones and laying them out rain hail and blistering wind. I google 'chain gang melbourne' and I find an article about the 'music band Chaingang' and a clever headline about chain restaurants. It helps to feel constant low-level indignation, I suppose, though I wonder about its overall effect on a person's health. I take beta-blockers to help with the general whiplash feeling in my body, tension of the mundane kind, my jaw tight and my sleep sleepless but I lie there anyway with my eyes closed waiting. In one episode of real chain gangs of Melbourne some prisoners (slaves?) from Pentridge village working in the mud field smashed their leg irons and made a run for it, five of them, and then another one who hadn't been in on the plan, Robert Taylor, seized the opportunity and bolted too, but he was older and slower and he ran in the wrong direction and by the time the guards knew it Robert Taylor was the only one within firing range so they shot him in the back, the bullet entering from the left side of his spine and exiting from the right breast, and afterwards someone wrote that 'the expression of his countenance was calm and serene, as though he had died without pain', what a hero, and what of the other five men, let's hope they ran and ran and found new names and something to fill out their days other than chipping boulders and laying stones, and who descends from these mavericks anyway, whose great-great-great-grandfather fled indentured labour and made life anew, if new life is possible, truly, in this old haunted land.

When I picture this scene, the mud, Robert Taylor, the gunshot, the pale shock on the faces of unshockable labourers, it takes place in the middle of Sydney Road in Coburg, it takes place right in front of where I spent every Saturday of my fifteenth year spruiking baby consumables out the front of Sam's Baby World. Like, good morning ladies and gentlemen; like, twenty per cent off all socks bibs and booties, this week only; like, come in, have a look around and get yourselves a bargain. At the spot an older Italian man, in his sixties maybe though fifteen-year-olds don't know a thing about age, always tried to get me to go out with him, and of course I refused him every week, I'm not that foolish, but I should admit that he bought me packs of Benson & Hedges Ultra Lights and I accepted these and I suppose that by accepting his gifts I was giving him horrible old-man permission to stay there talking at me week after week. This older Italian man, pleasingly slim for his age but his suit dull and dirty, filled me with dread. My every Saturday was governed by the fresh horror that he'd come by and demand my attention, and so it was to my great surprise that later, many years later, he appeared in my middle eye as I touched myself, short glimpses and imprecise, he's on his knees head bowed with his hand up my skirt, like he's praying me, or I'm lying down in the back of his car and he's begging me to let him eat me, so full of lust, and while I understand in this unwelcome fantasy I don't have a choice, I laugh nervously and then I climax, pulsing with shame.

For a long time I didn't know that some people chose where they lived, I assumed you just moved some-where and you found the cheapest house on the market and you moved in, a fresh start some real beginning and the house was always haunted by traces of a before, before the beginning, but you put up some paintings and some kid photos and slowly it became home. There were clues this was not the case for all people, for instance I was once in the car with a friend's dad, who was in effect a house flipper, as he pointed out the real-estate pockets that were already plush and the ones that were crap, and he said you'd want to buy somewhere in between, as though we—his daughter and I—would ever be in the position to choose, because years later he turned away his good daughter and not for any reason I ever understood. You don't want to be the first gentrifier, he implied, safer to be in the second wave and do a decent job of it. I knew about rich people and the middle classes because sometimes I was those things but usually not, but I didn't get it, choosing, until now that I pay real money, professional spec, to live in a kind of nice-enough house within a couple of kays of where I went to high school because of my aforementioned parochial connection to it. I am a consumer(!) paying for the choice to live where I believe I am at home. I can't see grass anywhere, native or otherwise, from the bench on my front porch, I can only see my neighbour across the road, a handsome but unhappy-looking middle-aged man living with his white-haired mother, oh well, great real estate, puffing at the pavement with his leaf blower, and I can see the other neighbours who live next door and all their visitors who come in and out in a way that suggests they are a bourgeois brand of drug dealer.

I dream a lot and good dreams too, meaty ones, but I never dream in nature, by which I mean I never dream I am in a great-outdoorsy setting unless I am being pursued by a human or a human force with terrible intentions. I've said it before and I'll say it again: non-human—extra-human—nature is terrifying, and I know there is something of a colonial legacy in this fact, which I am comfortable admitting; I have seen *Picnic at Hanging Rock*. When I was little and I lived in the country with my parents, neither of them much connected to land outside the city yet into things like growing veggies, they'd take us bush-walking because they wanted us to know about the world beyond tarmac and bourgeois drug dealers and meat-pie fog, and from this slice of childhood I remember useful facts about the bush, about treating nettle stings and how to behave around a snake, and I remember how Mum sounded singing cooee from the bottom of a canyon, me glowing with joy unadulterated, but still I am scared of the bush because I never spent long enough there to feel at home, just as I am still scared of the ocean, just as I am scared when I am at home alone at night, no human noises next to me, and I think of my house, the house I rent, built long before I was born, and I imagine the reptiles round it sunning themselves and spiders and birds everywhere, and it's the painful thought, or perhaps it's just boring, that I'm too tender for nature, not tough enough to unwind amid the sounds and dangers of animal chaos, and while I'm not phobic about snakes I am attacked by a snake in many of my dreams, but then I am told that these dreams are not about snakes at all, they're about men. And perhaps fear of nature is fear born of the sense that civilisation was supposed to make things easier and in many ways it does but the cost is very high, maybe fatal, for nature as well as for women, and the snakes, which are a placeholder for masculine triumph over everything, is what is destroying me incrementally is what is destroying, you know, nature.

...

There was a time when I felt very powerless, I was a young woman and so that's natural and I had chosen a profession that was always going to be difficult technically and financially and also hard on the ego, and one day an activist whose work I had reviewed and mildly criticised made contact and said we needed to talk about it, and this was kind, this real-life coffee scenario where a person older than me and more powerful took my words seriously enough to want to go beyond the internet warfare, and we had a falafel at the Half Moon Café and we got along in a way that we could get along because I accepted most of what he said and I didn't yet know that I wasn't always required to give my time and assent to men or perhaps more precisely people who looked down on me in a neutral, natural enough way, and then he announced lavishly that he had moved into my old neighbourhood, and the way he romanticised it really pissed me off, the way he was proud of himself for moving into this bleak place and the implication that this was rather transgressive of him and I said, yeah that's where my folks live, but he ignored me as male activists are wont to do and went on to explain its working-class history, the dairies that used to be there, how cool, and I thought briefly about how this phase of gentrification was the worst one, the phase where the newcomers' stakes in a place are purely accumulative, accumulative of some minuscule capital based on perceived riskiness, and sure, this guy moved in because he was an activist and an artist and he probably couldn't afford to live anywhere else, but still it's not *cool* it's sad and it's forgotten and when you live there, really live there, it's annoying that it's ages to the nearest corner store and frankly the absence of street lights is a public health and safety issue.

After school in the slow suburban afternoons I'd jump on the 19 and take it all the way home, and one day, bowing under the weight of my nerd-sized backpack, I walked home past a heavily armed police unit out the front of the blonde-brick flats by the train line, they hadn't even closed off the street, just cops in black standing there on a bright afternoon, long guns cocked. Not long before that, the night my little brother breakdanced at a school concert—he did the worm, which was a hit with the parents—Lewis Moran was shot to death one hundred metres away. I guess this was awful in all the ways anyone can imagine, but you can't deny the community-building aspect of a local gang killing, especially when it's old hardened career crims with beef and it doesn't really affect your life aside from the police tape blocking the passage to the fish and chip shop. People were *out* that night, then later we were all on the phone comparing our near-misses with the murderous underworld, attracted as we were to the animal qualities it promised: the treachery, the callousness, the sheer brazenness of murdering someone in public, during peak hour no less. And though most of the killings now are not related to this underworld story, it's still a hot topic at parties, stories about a friend who moved into a West Brunswick sharehouse and discovered false walls and secret rooms, you'd think it was the nouveau riche suburbs of New Jersey—how desperate we were for this gangland story to stick, for it to make real the cinema of crime, when in most instances crime was just kids bottling each other at the pub or your TV getting pinched in the night or men trying to force you into their cars so they could hurt you just as they do everywhere. Some people call the whole of Australia a Crime Scene because of what started here over two hundred years ago, but this Crime Scene isn't glamorous or attractive, because unlike the drive-bys and the Morans we're all, settlers at least, a little bit implicated in it. And then, around the time of the underworld gangland renaissance, Howard's terror laws passed and it became frightening to think what could happen to you, well, not you if you were an Anglo, but what could happen to you in the collective sense if you overstepped some undefined line of political propriety particularly if you were an Arab and I can't comment on this further because the fear for me was never material except to say that there was a feeling in the air and that feeling was powerlessness.

...

When I was at uni and trying to pay off a big debt I worked all kinds of jobs, mainly at bars and restaurants, under-the-table jobs for under the legal wages, and one of my jobs was at a shisha bar. I'd clean the shisha pipes out the back and pack them with apple mint strawberry tobacco for non-drinking teens and slice up melon and white cheese and pour black coffee for the owner of the bar and his friends. The owner's wife taught me how to stew bulgur and pack it in hollowed-out zucchinis. The bar didn't make any money, as in, we'd sell enough shishas and bitter black coffees to pay my wages for a shift, forty dollars, but little else, yet the owner spent every evening in there with his friends, sitting around, speaking only in Turkish. My boss was polite to me and with only a hint of condescension, I think he enjoyed having me there playing the role of personal assistant, I was a young girl in his palace there to make him hot drinks on command and follow other mundane instructions—go and puff up those cushions, wipe down the leaves of the indoor plants, bleach every glass object in the building. And one of the men who spent time there was my age, maybe his uncle or older brother forced him to come along, but he'd get bored and come over to the coffee bar and talk with me. At one point we swapped numbers and went out for shisha just me and him and he told me: credit-card fraud and importing drugs. He didn't tell me which drugs. But. That is how I came to learn I was a domestic worker in the headquarters of an organised crime outfit and it was just as well that I don't speak Turkish because otherwise I might have become an accessory.

When we were kids in the country for the full experience my city parents did things like send us out horse riding a few times and now I am terrified of the power of horses to really dominate the human spirit. One of the riding teachers had a Grandma Gladys, who lived across the street from us. Her pony, old Bluey, spent most of her time alone in a square paddock, so my parents offered to take Bluey off Gladys's hands and put her in our small backyard in town. We took Bluey home and rode her bareback barefoot round the streets like we were in *Puberty Blues* and Mick our fat-ish blue cattle dog would come out with us too no leash necessary real white-trash style. Well, one day someone left the side gate open and Bluey escaped and ran all the way home and Mum got in the Toyota Crown '72 and followed her and the punchline is that the pony went round the roundabout the right way. If there is always a question, and I believe there is, in this case it is this: where is home and what is freedom. The promise we accept is that freedom is the freedom to make ourselves anew, but in our hearts we are running home, running the right way round the roundabout, so is freedom the freedom to have a home even if home is a fenced-in square of lonely grass.

I was seeing a girl recently and while she lay on my bed she glanced around and she said, it looks like you could pack this place down with twenty-four hours' notice, and of course it's true because we are all itinerants now and everything I own now is three chairs a desk a bed frame a bookshelf two lamps I'd like to hold on to heaps of candles and two items of IKEA furniture that I'd happily leave on the pavement and never look back. Because IKEA inspires disgust in me maybe in the same way that Macca's inspires disgust in the bourgeoisie, because IKEA furniture is first of all ugly, but the ugliness is connected to its greatest sin, which is the implication its owners are not sticking round, they are international students who will never get residency they are backpackers living on twenty bucks a day they are sessional academics meeting their students in the corridor they are asylum seekers on Temporary Protection Visas they are renters in investment properties not homes for living in they are students always in a state of becoming they are contractors not employees so that their maladies are *their* problem they are their maladies which will kill them in their service to being they are flat-pack coffin-ready bodies. And if you think I'm joking just go up to your nearest IKEA object and press on it at a difficult angle and watch its injury insult the substance of your life.

I am not a sentimental person but yesterday I cried like a fool talking to my best friend who now lives in Detroit, I cried when I realised she'd never knock on my window again just because she was bored at her mum's place down the road because now she has got another life, and anyway her mum moved to Epping last year and my folks moved out to Werribee and one of my brothers and his family live in New York City and the other brother and his partner are still down the street but we don't hang out so much and all the people that signify that I have a home at all are scattered around the globe around the burbs and the only thing stable is my belief, rock solid, in the redemptive power of the hot twins who work at the bakery down the road, A1, who have worked there forever and who demonstrate little interest in their customers beyond doing a serviceable job of bringing out the falafels and the pies. That's supposed to be a joke but humour fails me when I think about it, me and my friend wagging school to get zaatar pizza there and other times after school to Barkly Square for hot chips and gravy, the gravy clearly not vegetarian, us sitting in the playground out the back, the yellow smell of dry grass cuttings, talking shit, and I mean that shouldn't be a reason to stay forever, I still plan to leave one day too, but now she lives in Detroit among playgrounds she never talked shit in with me while eating carbohydrate-rich foods and I'm leaving soon as well, and who knows maybe I won't come back either.

Allen Ginsberg

I nearly bought a second-
hand copy of *The Fall of
America* by Allen Ginsberg
because I thought it would
help me
learntowritepoetry.

I didn't buy it: it was
twenty euros, which
was probably fair but a bit
much for me right now.
Though later I spent more
money than that getting
drunk with my boyfriend.

At the bar I bought a
woman a glass of wine and
told her I was a waitress/
poet. Her fourth-language
tic was to say
yesyesyesyesyesyesyes all

inaline once she had
translated into German the
words I was using to spin
my bullshit.

My priorities are all
outofline.

Instead I bought a book of
Boris Pasternak's writings
printed before the wall
came down, stark cover design
for four euros. I liked the
cover, on which there
was a quote, '…the only
thing in our power is to
avoid distorting the voice
of life which sounds within
us'.

My lover from a year ago
drew a line around her
bedroom to protect it from
me, its boyish
mattressonthefloor, her
jeans tight on her tender. I
didn't love her enough to
HalobyBeyoncé her. She
didn't stay over at my

place the first time, which
my best friend said was
inexcusable.

I am trying to
learntowritepoetry because
my lover from a year ago
wrote poems about me,
using my words, and I felt
I don't know I felt like...
I have started
calling myself a poet in public—
I felt that she nailed my
terrible and not my tender.
+ because I hate essays.
+ because I keep fighting with
        editors, like. I went
        to high school I
        think I know what a
        question mark is?
+ because the comfort
        of grammar false freedom.

Instead I want revenge.
Anne Carson: 'As if anger
could be a kind of vocation
for some women. / It is a
chilly thought.'

...

The 'voiceoflife' which
sounds within me.

Allen Ginsberg is one of
those poets I suspect
may not be uncancellably
perfect yet he influenced
me inordinately. The
queer yet regressive
socialist type (I can't help
myself). Because before I
decided to think harder about not
failinguniversity, I was a
waitress/poetess. Before,
also, I saw that all the
other poetesses stand up

before one another to read
out loud, serious-voiced,
hand gestures wild and
rippling bodies. Which I
found shockingly
unappealing.

Once I tried to smoke opium
with a poet whose
number one hit poem
was about the streets of our city
burning. *The streets are on*

fire, he'd shout, or *The city
is burning*, I don't recall,
and all the others at the
bar hearing this would
whoop while I felt the
every cell jam
up in my body. We didn't
get high because the
opium was made poorly
from a hippie friend's
garden.
IthinkIfeelsomething?

His eyebrows were like
McDonald's arches and his
mission was romance.

I slept over but chastely
and he said when I awoke
he said I wanted to wake
you up with oral. Oh.
I don't know. He bought
me a mango. I took a
photo of him in bed
blackandwhite in his undies but never
got the film developed.
Poetry was fun.

...

Instead of me he got with
an artist whom he thought
I'd love and I did in fact I
was lustful but afraid of
women then.
I saw her at the gym her
perfectbody.

The story was that she'd
scream so loud when they
screwed that the
neighbours thought
murder. I mean the things
other women's boyfriends
tell you once they think
you are oneofthem.

What can I say. I never
loved any of you.

My lover from one year
ago is a great poetess. I
think her poems are funny.
My boyfriend thinks
they're sad. But in a good
way. Maybe he is jealous, I
mean what if I
fallforawoman again. They
say in TV shows and the

like that it's 'about the
person' but truly women
are totally different. Better
and worse at the same
time. I like how imprudent
guys are. They say 'you can
hook up with girls if you
want to' then when you do
they flip out. It's pathetic,
which means it's both
touching and couldkillyou.

The truth is I am averse to
narratives of pure romance
in the way that I am averse
to the avant-garde. In the
sense that I am averse to
that which is removed
from its context. Poetry is
often this. So is
critical theory. Sorry.

On the news I saw
the dead body of a gunman.
Supine mass of sinew.
Warm blood almost
stillnow in its veins, a
journalist gazing hawklike
from above. Watching this

I stretched my right
forearm to ease the
delicate tendon within.
Things outside the closed
glove of language. Like
slow-moving blood. Like
looking from above.

Amiri Baraka said that art
is the endless expression of
birth. Revolution is matter
transformed by
consciousness. Things like
          hot eruption of word
          jism from which the
          living
          being produced
          ecstatic fire interior
          life will always exist
          we settle for being
          craftsperson that
          devils use to drink
          blood
          art must be used as a
          weapon as the weapon
          against the rule to be
          cynical
          grasp the class
          struggle the

                    struggle for
                    production against
                    so-called writersblock
                    poetry is independent
                    of our
                    will
He said these things in
such a way I felt compelled to
set fire to my apartment.

I did not
set fire to my apartment.
But I gave myself over again
to the saint life of asceticism.
No more straitjacket
metaphors. No more
superego shadows cast over.
Confidence in *art* to *drink blood*,
no, *struggle*.

This is selfish but. I wish
sometimes that I could get
bent all the time.
Start drinking at
lunch and not stop till I
pass out at six. This is not
the kind of thing you tell
your therapist. If I had a
therapist I would not tell

her that. Instead I'd
impress her with self-
interrogation. Recover a
childhood moment after
which anything I did,
_____ would hate me still.
You'd make a great
therapist, she'd say. And
I'd run home to empty out
another wine bottle. Hide
the empties in. The oven.

You'd be surprised how
unscathed I really
am. Like a seal.

I have begun
again to
chew
nicotine gum.

Unwed Teen Mum Mary

I'm trying to get work taste-testing new snacks for 7-Eleven. They pay forty dollars per taste-test in the form of a prepaid Visa gift card, which will be handy for buying groceries or topping up my myki. To apply to be a person to whom 7-Eleven offers such precious opportunities, I must fill out a questionnaire in such a way as to convince their marketing people that I am a frenetic consumer of overpriced snacks.

In the questionnaire, I select the statement 'I work to live', which is *true,* but only in the sense that to pay for the debt of living a person is required to work. This is not a 'choice' so much as a banality.

...

'How often do you make impulse purchases at 7-Eleven stores?' the questionnaire asks.

'Frequently,' I lie. In fact I hate 7-Eleven and everything in it, in fact I almost never impulse-buy convenience-store products.

Yesterday I applied for work running platters of canapés at the catering company I worked for when I was twenty. Yesterday I signed up to a mailing list for market-research opportunities. Yesterday I asked my friends with kids to pass my number on to any wealthy parents they know who are looking for help with child care or cleaning. Yesterday I applied for work counting votes in the upcoming state election.

An editor emailed the other day, asking if I would contribute to her anthology on abortion, something with the word 'choice' in the title, which would raise funds for a national non-profit abortion provider. She said I'd get paid for my contribution. I thought about the kind of anthology this would be, and how the kind of anthology this would be was probably the kind of anthology I would pay little attention to—though I was flattered to be asked to contribute to it—because I am basically a snob, and because I don't think that politicians intent on restricting or criminalising reproductive rights need to read a nuanced anthology on abortion written by mostly white, mostly middle-class women like me so much as they need to be taken out one at a time. A joke. That's a joke. And then I thought about the number of 7-Eleven taste-tests I'd have to do for the same amount of money, how many hours of running platters

of canapés to hotel corporation stakeholders on Cup weekend.
I chose the two hundred dollars.

When I think about the word 'choice' I think about how it
represents a fantasy. An important fantasy and one, perhaps,
worth protecting, but an unreal circumstance, really. 'Circumstances,' writes Anne Boyer, 'are the stage on which agency
performs.' Agency as opposed to autonomy, which requires
some degree of control over circumstances. For example, I didn't
choose to be alive and I didn't choose to be settled in an overpriced city and I didn't choose at age thirty to be lying about my
love of Slurpees to pay for groceries from one of the duopoly of
price-fixing supermarkets , groceries I cook up at my house that
also serves as my primary workspace where I work at my several
not-really-real jobs, and I didn't choose to carry around a small
robot that exposes me to radiation and listens to all of my words
and bodily excretions—well, perhaps I did choose that purchase,
naive consumer me, but without it my several not-really-real jobs
would fast become unviable.

—Siri, do I have a choice?
    —*I really couldn't say, Ellena.*

I didn't choose my parents and they didn't choose me—they
didn't choose my particular genetic code nor my penchant for
feeling hard done by nor my rather negative attitude towards
the hegemony of biological family-making. I didn't choose
to be a person who finds intolerable things that other people, most people—normal people—tolerate seemingly with

pleasure and with ease. Things like handing over personal data to corporations in exchange for small product bonuses. Things like wedding registries. Things like the legal enforcement of helmet-wearing.

I didn't choose to get pregnant when I did, though I was complicit in the choice in that I chose to have sex that night, I suppose, in the mangled way that sometimes happens with a person you have not planned to have sex with and probably won't again, and I chose to have it in such a way that made possible a slippage of biological material from one place to another, though in all honesty I didn't think that the person I was with would be so careless or cruel as to endanger me in that way, and I chose to imbibe the several drinks that led me to this somewhat unglamorous affair. I did not choose the patriarchal condition of normative heterosexual hook-ups whereby the primary form of eroticism is the careless penile penetration of women and woman-shaped people in pursuit of male orgasm regardless of the risk of disease or pregnancy, but I did choose to exercise in my warped way my puny young-girl agency to 'objectify' guys with the aim of reversing the ways in which I had been fucked and fucked over by them.

I didn't choose to be too broke to pay the out-of-pocket for the abortion anaesthetic, which at the Royal Women's was a hundred and forty dollars, and I didn't choose the character of the girl I was seeing at the time, though the character of the girl I was seeing at the time was what had endeared her to me, and while I did not choose for her to pay for the anaesthetic, she did it anyway, because that was her character, and while I was getting my guts pried open the girl napped on her rolled-up leather jacket like a sweet punk-rock baby in the barren chamber of the hospital, and for this she is due my eternal gratitude.

I didn't choose to have zero emotional after-effects from that abortion, though I felt I couldn't mention this too often or too loudly in case it seemed in some way to trivialise the emotional after-effects others experienced after theirs. More trivialising, I think, is the dominant cultural narrative I choose now not to abide by, the narrative of inevitable future shame and regret post abortion, as though a feeling of regret is worse than a life-time of poverty, or being eternally tethered to a man you hate, or being dependent for years on a biological family you wish to be separate from, or simply being forced to do something you instinctively don't want to do. I regret a lot, believe me: I regret my poor food choices and my poor work choices and I regret being born with the biological equipment that bears the burden of poor sexual choice-making under the influence of alcohol at age twenty. But in no chamber of my soul is there an inkling of regret about ending a pregnancy I did not want, and if I hadn't had the legal choice to end it at the Royal Women's I'd have done it anyway, I'd have rolled down a flight of stairs, I'd have seen a dodgy doctor, I'd have drunk poison, I'd have done it all, and I might have died trying.

Because this is what agency is: it is doing what you can do with the circumstances you are dealt. It is choosing to do what you need to do, even and especially when your parents or your superego or the law disapproves. In my opinion, sex is not a sacred jewel, and poor erotic decisions are not something women need protection from, and motherhood is not holy. In my view, any effort to pair femininity with maternity with biological destiny with virgin births with earthy crystal-lovemaking is an effort to relegate the female form to a position of inferiority, to a state of constant need and gratitude and dependence.

It's all predicated on a founding myth of Christian society, the ideal of sexless maternity. But Julia Kristeva writes that the 'virgin' of the Virgin Mary was in fact a mistranslation of an ancient Semitic word for unmarried young woman. Conflating 'virgin' with 'unmarried young woman', she says, erases the young mother's extra-patriarchal *jouissance*, evidence of her bodily joy and her sensual desires, and subsumes it under the sign of the male-controlled 'virgin'. The mistranslation is said to strip pre-Christian societies of their matrilineal inheritance rites, and it strips Mary of her agency, too—her scampish, light-filled, unwed spirit—and replaces it with the sign of the father.

In other words, if the Virgin Mary had more correctly been named the Unwed Teen Mum Mary, we who inherit the moral framework of the Christian tradition might not feel compelled to trot out our *narratives*, our evidence that access to safe and affordable abortion is a moral good in that it is a material good in that there can be no moral good without humans exercising their agency in whatever piddling ways they can. Sexuality and impurity might not be coupled. Maternity might be understood as just one of the many ways a person can choose to belong to time rather than as a duty women with wombs have to tip themselves completely into the wellbeing and service of others.

It is also true, however, that we who have inherited the moral framework of the Christian tradition have inherited a limited set of tropes through which we understand what a body is and what a gender does, and from within this fog we find it challenging or perhaps inconvenient to look upon the full force of the animal urges that course through us all. The animal spirit that offers recourse to say no, to say I will not abide, to say I will choose the smallest thing that has been offered to me, to protect me, to protect the others whose tender red organs have been taken, in name and in law, away from the law of their own agency.

At twenty I did not want to be someone's mother. At thirty I have been all kinds of mother: I have paid the rent for rock-dogs, I have made more meals than have been made for me, I have given more pleasure than has been given me, I am practically a saint, but no one tells me that, not enough anyway, though I am trying again to choose to not do that, to not be a mother.

Instead I'm trying to see that my tender red organs and the few dollars I earn and the words that I say and write are truly mine and that I'm therefore responsible for what I do with them. Sheila Heti writes that the hardest thing for a woman to do is to choose to not become a mother, and while the hardest thing is not always the best thing I am curious about a life where choice is more rigorously available to me and perhaps the first choice to make is the choice to take my agency take it make it mine.

...

'What do you love most about 7-Eleven stores?' the question-naire asks me.

'The convenience,' I reply. 'And the charming service I always receive! :)'

Holidays with Men

When I was starting out writing my own stuff, I published a series of vignettes titled 'Holidays with Men' in a zine that a guy from uni put together. I read at the zine's launch, which was held upstairs at a gentrified East Brunswick bar: bare walls, aluminium stacking stools, tall, bright windows. It was a damp white afternoon. A few friends came along.

The day of the launch, I felt more self-conscious than usual. I had recently gained

Coins

I had never met a man with such a coordinated sense of Englishness about him. He left the house in a tweed hat, a tweed coat and, if my memory serves me, a tweed tie, though this detail seems like overkill. He wore leather gloves to drive around town in his little hatchback. He was my grandfather and he loved me, even though we'd never met. I was eighteen. He was small and seventy-something. On the walls of his home hung school photographs of my brothers and me, which my mother had been sending him, in secret, for years. He had not seen my father, his son, in fifty years.

At lunch at the pub, he told me the regret of his life. I didn't want this confession, it was too sad for me to bear, but I listened. He had not been a father to his son. They had been too young, he said, when they had him; they would never have made it. And then the migration severed all chances of a reunion. As he told me of his heartbreak, his body moved just like my father's. I couldn't get it out of my head. He was my father, accelerated in time. I didn't want his sadness, I was too young, but I opened myself to it.

When he stood up to pay, he shook the waiter's hand, and slipped into it two two-pound coins.

Lighthouse

We bickered the whole way along the beach and through the pretty shrubs in the way holidaying couples who will not stay together very long

weight—quickly, I thought, and without grace. I felt hideous and ungainly and I didn't yet know how to wear clothes on the new parts of my body. I was newly single, too, in a desperate and deplorable kind of way— desiring but spurning any and all attention. The store I worked at had recently cut my shifts down to the barest minimum. So I was broke, too. I was a pitiable character. I didn't feel like parading stories from my love life in front of a small crowd of artsy people; clearly I was a troll who did not deserve a love life.

I remember what I wore that day, possibly because of photographic evidence that hung around on my social media for years afterwards: a long-sleeved grey top and a waist-high blue cotton skirt; an outfit that was supposed to create the illusion of a slim waist but in fact exaggerated the opposite. I was nervous. I didn't take a beta-blocker before the performance (I didn't know about beta-blockers yet). As I read, my hands shook. At a dramatic moment, one that made mention of a death I had not yet integrated, I swallowed my saliva so as to not burst out a sob. The sob I repressed was not, as the audience might have inferred, a sob of sadness, but one of sheer embarrassment. Nobody who attended that launch could argue that this reading went well.

After the reading, I stood with my housemate James, feeling mortified. Two guys approached. The one with glasses and a smooth brown face was full of praise.

'Thank you,' I said. 'Thanks.' And excused myself to go to the bar. James followed me. He said, 'If you wanna meet someone, Ellena, you'll have to let them talk to you first.'

The break-up that preceded 'Holidays with Men' was with someone I'd been with for a couple of years. Not the longest time, but I was shattered. The romance had been predicated, I now realised, on a fantasy of the transformative power of travel and of love realised in the realm of the intellect. In the very beginning of the romance, I had followed him on his research trip to Papua New Guinea and are prone to, protracted arguments which are, perhaps, designed to bring the couple closer by testing the limits of their love, but are in fact simply exhausting. We had been walking all afternoon, looking for a famous lighthouse, famous in part because it had somehow not been bombed by the Germans. Between us we had ten euros for the rest of the trip— another twenty-four hours—and we were both *so hungry*. But I knew that because he was male and tall, he'd get to eat more of whatever food we could afford to buy (a loaf of bread and a family-sized pack of orange Cheetos). On the way back, we had sex on the cold beach for no reason other than to up the romance factor, despite the fact it wasn't all that pleasurable and we were not exactly having a romantic time. He took a photo of me that turned out sort of pretty, right at the spot where we did it. I know, now, not to get envious of other people's holiday snaps because although in the photo I am smiling, so happy, I was in a vile mood that lasted until we played Scrabble that night, where I cheated, banking on the fact that he was not a native English speaker. Words like 'moted' and 'peb', which are not real words in the English language but sound like they could be.

Denzel

He and I walked all the way along Venice Beach to where it becomes more like Santa Monica, where the hustlers spoke to us in French because we looked foreign, I suppose, or because both of us were wearing Lacoste. We lay next to each other on the fake-green grass and took photos up close because that's how we wanted to remember each other forever, basking in clear light and love. Then we went and saw that terrible Denzel movie because it was on and we had time to kill, and even the security guard at the cinema agreed that it was 'a bit sanctimonious'.

Truck Stop

We decided on a week in the flower mountains. Get out of the city. Get him away from hard drugs. I had just

to Japan. This man was a charming and quite brilliant person, but complicated in ways that are often concomitant with charm and brilliance. The failure of the relationship presented itself to me as a single failure containing within it all other failures. After the break-up I didn't yearn for this ex-boyfriend. I resented him. The shattering was instead of a narrative kind. It marked the end of a trick vision I had designed for my young life.

For example. Why did I go after him? An instinct for competition. Other women had wanted him (or so he said) and so I did, too. What did I want from him? Access to a social class I had not been invited into. Travel—for a purpose. He'd experienced a cultural and economic mobility that I hoped to replicate. Why did I stay with him long after I got, or didn't get, what I hoped for? A fantasy needs an application to prove itself unreal.

A year after 'Holidays with Men' was published in that little magazine, an acquaintance wrote to me saying that she'd found a copy and had recognised herself in one of my vignettes.

The acquaintance had been one half of a couple on the rocks I had met and dined with in New York City. During the dinner, and drinks afterwards, they'd had a public, and dramatic, falling-out. I wrote about it in 'Holidays with Men' jokingly, frivolously, as in: *look* at these *out* of *control people*. I'd reduced this couple, strangers almost, to characters in a nasty little play. My acquaintance wrote about how damaged and damaging that relationship had been for her, and how reading about it from someone else's perspective stung.

It hadn't crossed my mind that a tiny nothing, printed on low-quality stock, could travel just as easily as my writing body had. An impression of a relationship not working. Too much bourbon. A fleeting encounter in a city that turns white with snow in winter. I was mortified. I had exposed this person, who hadn't wronged me in any way, to the awfulness of having been written about. An experience that is all the more horrible because its humiliation is lined with the egoistic delight in being written

quit my magazine job. We made our way to the back of the night bus as it stumbled into gear just before dusk, sat ourselves down in the corner sleeper seats. As the bus yawned out of view of the city's brilliant lights, I pulled a bottle of rum from my bag. Hours passed. We talked. We held each other. We crashed.

When, at three a.m., a truck smashed into the rear corner of the bus, a foot from my head, he and I were asleep. Confusing, then, to awake covered in a film of powdered glass, heavier shards of it dispersed across my body. I drew a hand to my face, which felt wet and gluey. Blood, lots of it, which didn't seem like mine. Which was mine. I turned to see him looking at me in horror.

Shit, I thought. I've lost my face.

I sat quietly, blood sticky on my hands, while he screamed at the bus driver to do something, give him something to mop it up. Together we cleaned my face with a wad of cotton wool and water from a bottle, and found the source of all that blood: a small gash just above my right temple. Deep and swollen, but not very wide.

At the truck stop, where all the passengers had to wait for a replacement bus, he looked at me very seriously and he said, 'The truck that hit us fell off the cliff.'

I peered into the dark. The road did not appear to be running along the edge of a cliff. I said nothing. He was famous for twisting the truth. Whatever happened to the truck, I would never know.

'I thought about giving you my shirt,' he said, 'to wrap around your head. But it's YSL.'

'Yeah, but it's ten-dollar YSL from the markets.'

Windows

From the couch, I watched a big blonde woman bring in her laundry from the balcony. I didn't mean to invade. It just happened; I was just… Looking. Through another window, across the way, I saw an older guy spread out on his couch watching the football, a can of Coke at his feet. His legs were outstretched, emphatically.

about. An illicit, almost sexual chill aroused by the twinning of exposure and shame. A shock of the obvious: that my body, my voice, my writing, had, in its public exhibition, a public dimension which equated to a responsibility.

'I will do anything to avoid boredom,' writes Anne Carson. 'It is the task of a lifetime.' I've travelled more than others in my family, though they are beginning to catch up. I've travelled more than many of my friends who have money. Still, I've been to few of the places I long to see. Not yet the Trans-Siberian. Not yet the Albanian coast. Not yet Karachi or Beirut or Johannesburg. A lot of effort to experience a simple sensation of out of place and out of time. There were moments in my twenties when I considered laundry powder 'too expensive' to justify its purchase, yet happily blew a fortnight's pay on a discounted fare to Indonesia. There were times when I lost part-time jobs because I wanted to go for weeks, or months, to a place where no one knew my name. It has been the task of a lifetime, avoiding boredom. Travel has, in a way, allowed me to avoid the cost of living.

Pierre Bourdieu writes that there is a spiritual dimension to 'cultural capital' (the social qualities that enhance class mobility in a stratified society). He writes that in cultivating rarefied artistic tastes, the upper-middle classes find 'a feeling of social flying'. I am no sociologist, but I might add to the sense of social flying the theme of travel. Literal flying. Soaring into spaces, uninvited, with the security that attends the privileges of disposable incomes and homes to return to. *Though 'homes to return to' are perhaps rarer than they once were.*

In the wake of Europe's devastation under fascism, Theodor Adorno wrote that 'dwelling, in the proper sense, is now impossible'. For Adorno, and the exiles and refugees like him, home was a long-gone fantasy. 'The best mode of conduct, in face of all this,' he wrote, 'still seems an uncommitted, suspended one.' And what could be less committed than a life of travel? Travel, in discourse, is a lack of

I wondered, does it get too much? Living in a real city, unlike spread-out suburban Australia? After forty years of half-clothed bodies in your line of vision do you think: enough! I'm moving to the country.

I couldn't imagine getting sick of it. The safety of knowing that other bodies were nearby.

A few days later, I sipped a cup of tea at the kitchen window, looking again, mindlessly, and a man across the way dropped his pants, hunched his thick shoulders over, and started masturbating. He was looking straight at me.

Baggage

Although I didn't yet have my L-plates, he let me drive almost the whole way interstate in his Commodore. When we got to his parents' house we were shown to his old room with two single beds, which later that night we pushed together and made love on with wide-mouthed kisses.

He took me to the top of the mountain to look at the bluest lake I've ever seen, a lake that radiates light at certain times of the year due to mysterious alchemy, and then we had dinner at a pub that had only one vegetarian option, with a guy whose brother had disappeared in India two years before. They talked a lot about how the search was going, not saying, both, what they didn't want to think about.

After dinner, he told me that he liked me so much because I had no baggage, which was true mainly because I was seventeen years old and he was almost a grown man.

Luxury Hotel

It was not the first luxury hotel room. There had been the Lupe Fiasco afterparty fiasco—we access-all-areas girls entered the smoke-filled room at the Marriott, and the chief groupie poured us each a vodka.

Where's Lupe? we asked.

We sipped from plastic glasses, sat nestled on couches piled high with overcoats, and waited. Loud music. Then, the chubby guitarist's hand on my leg. And the danger sliding like oil on the lips of the bassist, who wore

commitment, even to the extent that it signifies a tainted, perhaps even immoral, movement of one kind of body from one place to another and back again home. That body is coded as white, usually, and male.

There are negative and positive frames to read discourses of travel through, writes the historian James Clifford. There is 'travel, negatively viewed as transience, superficiality, tourism, exile, and rootlessness'; and there is 'travel positively conceived as exploration, research, escape, transforming encounter'. In either iteration of travel, positive or negative, its language is limited; its presumed subject is free in ways that people, en masse, in history, have largely not been. And yet, as Clifford points out, for every little lord on his Grand Tour there was his team of servants: people carrying his cases, cooking his meals, perhaps even catering to his sexual wants. Were they not travellers, too?

Travel is not just tours of the Grand or Contiki variety. Travel is connected to migration, to economics, to security.

Who travels? Tourists, of course. Who else? Pilgrims, sports fans, seasonal workers, touring artists, international students, parents visiting children who live in the city, children of migrants meeting grandparents for the first time, scholars, soldiers, miners, voluntourists, sailors, truckers, emergency workers, retired English nurses living out divorcée twilights in Mallorca, economic migrants returning to their cities of birth after decades away, carrying with them tartan bags bursting with medicines and blankets. A traveller might return home; she might not. A return, to paraphrase Heraclitus, may not be possible. The traveller is not a migrant, though, writes Iain Chambers, a scholar of cultural and postcolonial studies. For the migrant, 'the promise of a homecoming—completing the story, domesticating the detour—becomes an impossibility'.

Although it was still in its early stages, the relationship started to unravel when we settled into daily life in PNG. He began to sink under the weight of his research project. Within weeks,

sunglasses inside and a terry towelling robe. Our faces drained when we realised that Lupe would not be coming to the party. The lights switched off quickly then, pitch darkness, me on my knees digging for my bag. Her tears in the corridor. And our escape.

So, not the first luxury hotel. But perhaps the first rental car? It was the early days and he wooed me. You know. Just a regular guy, staying at luxury hotels for academic conferences. My dreams of our coupling. Every email I composed to him had an eagle eye on posterity.

We arrived at the conference late, large sunglasses on.

'You sure know how to do a conference,' someone said as we stepped out of the rental car. As he delivered an incomprehensible paper, I read the news. As he debated with his seniors, I stepped out for a constitutional. In the evening, we met with some of the academics he knew for a drink. My first encounter with them, the teachers, not as a student. One of them hated his wife but loved his baby. Another insisted that everyone drink the same overpriced, swamp-flavoured whiskey he was ordering for himself. One of them, I saw over his shoulder, had twelve thousand dollars sitting in his everyday bank account, which was an amount of money I had never considered existing all in one place. That was, I think, the beginning of my education.

The Swan

While he was in the shower, I used his phone to check my email. Maybe I looked through his messages while I was there. Maybe I read something I wasn't supposed to. Maybe I lacked discretion and I blurted out, *who is she?* He yelled about privacy and his phone. Which I suppose he was right to. But.

The one time I went to his hometown with him, he took me to the Swan. Said it was his old local. We went there several nights in a row. A friend, rich from mining business, plied us with mid-strength beers. Said to me, 'I didn't expect a feminist to look like you.'

'Whatever do you mean?' I asked.

his sparkle dimmed; he stayed in bed longer and longer. His supervisor had warned him about taking a partner to the field. Apparently, the wisdom goes, partners don't fare well in isolated foreign environments with nothing to do and no one to talk to. But I'm a writer, I said. I always have something to do. A woman from the women's council I talked to knew a man who was looking for help from a writer to write his life story. I met with him one day and he looked at me in a way I knew about. The man was not an innocent, and, at twenty-four, neither was I. I introduced myself as my boyfriend's fiancée. The man laughed. Clearly, I was not. Clearly, my boyfriend and I had just met. I was talking to a man who had been to prison and broken out of it a freedom fighter. Had lived through a heinous civil war. Had travelled through every town and village in the archipelago. Spoke a handful of languages. Was a polygamist, with designs on chiefdom. Here was a worldly man, much worldlier than I, and I had thought I might offend him by admitting that

I 'lived in sin' with this skinny man who was struggling to finish his PhD.

Travel, in the broadest sense possible, encompasses the furthest reaches of a culture. Networks driven by survival, by desire, by a twinning of the two, have flung bodies and stories away from homes for all of history, and all of prehistory, too. These movements make history. They make history history.

Discourse, writes the author Samuel R. Delany, 'is what tells us what is central and what is peripheral—what is a mistake, an anomaly, an accident, a joke'. Discourse is what insists that a traveller is a decadent and thoughtless tourist. Or a foolish seeker of enlightened truths, which he will never find (*wherever you go...*). Perhaps that is correct; or that one iteration of travel is corrupt beyond redemption. Discourse (Delany again) 'tells us what to pay attention to and what to ignore. It tells us what sort of attention to pay. It tells us what is anomalous and therefore nonserious.' Therefore: what else.

...

That night I counted eight pints down his throat, though it might have been more, and afterwards he drove me home. I didn't want to get in the car.

'How else are you going to get home?' he said.

I didn't know where I was.

We'd been fighting, starting to fight. I wanted to go home, he wanted to keep pounding beers. There was no point in being left alone in the middle of wherever. So I got in.

On the highway, he weaved between lanes and other cars, the puddles of light on the tarmac slipping quicker and quicker beneath us. I looked at the faces of other drivers as we passed them, their eyes mad with alcohol, too. I screamed at him to let me out. Over and again I said, 'I'll get an Uber! I don't care if it's a hundred dollars.'

'There are no Ubers out here,' he screamed back.

He laughed, then, in a way that reminded me of Al Pacino playing the devil in the 1997 horror-comedy *The Devil's Advocate*.

Later, at his mum's house, I cried and cried. He wrestled me in his rage and placed his body on top of mine, pinning me down. His mother busted into the room to tell us to stop.

It was at the Swan, another time, months or maybe a year later, a time when I wasn't there, with a person whose name he'd never mentioned. But its traces were there on his phone.

Probably I had seen it coming.

Green Lake

She and I disrobed at the edge of the water, slid beneath the emerald surface. Once we were immersed in the dark green pool, he ran down the bank, stripped to his undies and hurtled in, too. It was two or three days before Christmas. We were in the North of Vietnam, one or two or three hundred kilometres from Hanoi. The water should have been chilly, but it wasn't. The water was warm like red wine served badly in summer. It thawed our skin as we rolled around in its stillness. As she lunged into a floating backflip her breasts, belly, thighs and finally her

The Egyptian tour guide who studied abroad, in Germany.

The Vietnamese would-be party girl whose passport blocks her from being flown on a drug-fuelled whim to Singapore by the international DJ.

The musician from Brisbane who falls in love with a gitano man and moves into his home, in a cave, studies flamenco, stays for six years.

Therefore: and.

Responsibility for this mass and unprecedented movement of bodies is assumed by the planet's precarious diversity. The cultural hierarchies imposed by tourism as a consequence of globalisation are all too clear. The destruction of locales and languages, of atavistic knowledge, of survival skills, delicacies, forms of pleasure and praise—the eradication of the particular under the careless heft of the commercial, the new universal.

I've moved about the planet in ways that seem anomalous, even wrong. Global economic inequality and a strong-enough Australian dollar. Cheap air

travel. Low personal expecta-
tions of comfort and security.
Precarious employment, and
months of no-income, when living somewhere other than my
city made fiscal sense. But doing
that alone, I exposed my form
to the possibility of its rape, its
murder. Its erasure. More time
away from networks of security.
More time in places without a
care in the world for me.

Violence, and the threat of it, provides the materials for one class
of people to extinguish another.
This asymmetry is formed first,
at conception, in the ideation
of male over female, masculine
over feminine. This asymmetry is replicated infinitely in all
other forms: adult over child,
landowner over tenant, human
over land, cis over trans, coupled
over single, person over animal,
capital over person, captor over
captive, invader over native,
unscrupulous over principled.
Every person who is not at risk
of extinction benefits from the
other's precarity. Even the nice
ones. Even the good ones. Even
the me, and the not me, too.

A threat is always real and unreal simultaneously. It is made

knees darted through the folds of
dark water. My joy deepened with
every turn.

They were a couple. Her, I'd
known since underage gigs: cow-
boy boots, bangs, love-me-please red
lipstick. He was her London-life
boyfriend: leather jacket, sixties
moustache, carrying about a look of
having been put upon.

The lake was so picturesque it had
the look of man-made perfection.
I have never since been able to locate
it on a map or online. I have to accept
that my memory is the only trace I
have of this afternoon. Or was it the
morning?

Sometimes the water is amaranth,
when I remember it. And the trees
lining its banks are forresty grey
pines with long soft needles, like fingers. Mostly I can agree with myself
that the water was green, green with
a sweet muddy flavour, and the foli-
age all around it was bamboo. The
heat emanating from the water concerned me, but only a little. I thought
of the blue-green algae that had given
kids pelican itch when we swam in

dams and lakes as a child. No one else was swimming there. Or fishing. Or washing.

Which made me think: odd. Contaminated? Or a reservoir. Or some kind of nature reserve?

Whatever it was, at least we're still alive.

She told me, years later, that he hurt her on that trip. I knew they had been fighting, but I wasn't there. Why wasn't I there?

It took us another day or two of motorcycling through twisting, chilly mountains to get back to the city, where we split up, went off to our respective hotels. When they got to their room, he hurt her.

At least, we're still alive.

material by how it structures experience. How women and queer people walk, speak, smile. What we do and say and where we allow our bodies to see and be seen alone. The threat and its indiscriminate actualisation encourages us to stay in, or to tacitly accept the risk: to spend energy considering how best to navigate danger. No amount of self-discipline can protect a person from her protector. One in ten women. The same number the Romans used to control their military platoons. It's called *decimation*. And, to seek protection—voluntarily or involuntarily—from men. And what a danger it is, to need a protector, and protection from that protector.

You Dirty Phony Saint
and Martyr

I was in the courtyard of a cafe in East London (£7.50 for my coffee and sandwich and some wifi) and the two waitresses working but not really *working* working were smoking cigarettes and drinking 'cheeky' juices at the table next to me. The one with false eyelashes and long, slim, honey-coloured limbs told the other about her seventeen-hour trip to Ibiza with Diplo, who was, for the weekend, her squeeze, where she had embarrassed herself by drinking four little bottles of red wine on the private jet, the purple of which Diplo had to wipe off her lips when she arrived. Before and after the show, she said, Diplo and his dancers drank green tea and ate quinoa salads because, for them, it wasn't a party, it was *work*. Of course, as a feminist, I saw her extravagant make-up and her limbs, taut despite the red-wine calories, as a kind of *work*, too: a work, at least, of imagination and of aspiration.

'Like, I used to have posters of Diplo on my wall as a teenager,' she said to her colleague. 'I couldn't imagine him even looking at me, you know? And then, there I was. On his private plane.'

A year before she died, Kathy Acker wrote in a notebook:

> Concerning imagination: At age 30 I was working in a cookie shop. There was absolutely nothing in the society that in any way made it seem possible for me to earn my living as a writer. I was, and still am, the most noncommercial of writers. I said, if X doesn't exist, you have to make it exist. You just imagine it…

Much has been said about how writers earn money writing when writing does not itself generate money; more will be said, too, of the nexus of power, privilege and prestige in literature, and I have little to add here. More interesting to me is that some artists, in fact, do it without networks of financial security. They do it because they are driven by desperate and belligerent ambition. They believe, at least in the beginning—they must—that they are the specials. ('I used to believe that I was exceptional and abnormal,' wrote John Berger.) Special enough to ask for more than they have been given.

There are many kinds of hunger. And when we are hungry, sometimes it is our own goddamn fault.

Last year I read a lot of Gertrude Stein and, while drenched in her odd, somewhat aggressive and sumptuous world, I'd teach my classes ($120 per hour) armed with printouts of her 'portraits'. If my students neglected to do their readings, I whipped her out as a form of punishment (of course, Gertrude Stein is no real punishment). During one such session, the brightest student—who every week arrived late and left early, holes in her tights, clearly hungover, yet in possession of an extraordinary brain—brought up Hemingway's 'lyric memoir' *A Moveable Feast*; brought up how, in it, Hemingway brutally criticised Stein. I'd gone through my Hemingway craze in high school, when I loved his languor and barely concealed petulance, but I hadn't returned to his work to see if I might still value his opinion. In any case, I had never read *A Moveable Feast* and couldn't comment on this accusation, except to declare in the classroom that autobiographies tend to reveal more about their authors than their authors know.

A little while later, I was invited to speak on a panel addressing my old university's new honours students, which was surprising, because I had done okay but not brilliantly in my honours year, which I had enrolled in, initially—and perhaps unbelievably—for the purpose of receiving the Austudy ($440 a fortnight) that I had never been able get before on account of multiple universe-not-aligning reasons. This meant my undergraduate years were pure hustle and debt until I came to edit the student newspaper ($17,000 per annum). After graduating I learned that not only was I terrible at earning money from writing, I was also an undesirable in the broader job economy. Following this revelation, I met J, a slightly older, slightly more affluent boy (yet frantically self-made), and I joined him overseas on his research trip. He paid for most of it on his meagre scholarship, so that took care of half a year or so, but still we were broke and mainly ate noodles and drank malt liquor instead of beer, and while he 'worked' on his project, or lay in bed consumed by guilt for not working on his project, I developed a fitness fanaticism and—when I wasn't running or doing weights—read a lot, and wrote some short pieces that brought in a few hundred here and there and in one case some prize money. But, really, what I needed was a living wage, and Austudy, at $440 a fortnight, sounded pretty plush, so the idea of returning to Melbourne to do my honours year was appealing, in that it would force me to write, and to write with seriousness as my goal.

After finishing the panel for the new students, I was handed a $50 bookshop voucher, which I promptly exchanged for a new Clairefontaine notebook ($6.95), another copy of Tom Cho's *Look Who's Morphing* ($24.95) to replace the one a friend had accidentally defaced, and *A Moveable Feast* ($16.95), though I didn't read *A Moveable Feast* until I was walking out on Melbourne and into a new life in Berlin ($500 sale fare, one way), where I thought it might be possible to live off what was now my PhD student stipend ($26,000 per annum) while writing a serious thesis, or, at least, a book. It was a strange sensation to read *A Moveable Feast* under these circumstances: to be in the process of establishing a writing life away from my social support structures and my comforts and my access to crappy temporary hospitality jobs when things went sideways, and to read the most commonly cited (and arguably most hackneyed) handbook on the topic.

Let's forget what Hemingway says about Gertrude Stein and, by extension, women as a class—'there is not much future in men being friends with great women although it can be pleasant enough before it gets better or worse, and there is usually even less future with truly ambitious women writers'—and instead think about him and Paris and money.

The Berlin decision and, in fact, every decision I have made so far in both my writing and love life, has, to some degree, been made with day-to-day money and future money in mind. For example: I guess I'd hoped, or imagined, that working as a volunteer for the literary journal the *Lifted Brow* for years (five) would accrue cultural capital that would morph into material capital, but it has not, yet, and might never, unless I wish to become a scholar of independent literary magazines, or edit a hypothetical one that pays a salary the fraction of what I could earn in a regular middle-class profession like teaching high-school students.

Aside from fearing great women and truly ambitious women writers in particular, Hemingway talks about living in poverty in Paris while learning to write; he speaks of a wretched sort of living, but a wretchedness tempered by the choice to make art, and this is summed up in a strange tale about child care.

In the spirit of candour, I should admit that while reading *A Moveable Feast* I imposed upon it my mean-spirited feminism; as I read, a little voice instructed me to ask: *who is looking after your baby, Hemingway, who is washing your socks? Presumably your WIFE, your suffering female companion, while YOU pursue YOUR INANE PASSIONS.* And while my instinct for framing and naming patriarchal behaviours is usually correct, in this case it was wrong.

Hemingway's wife at the time, Hadley, is a pianist; after Ernest goes off to the cafe to work, she trundles down to her studio, coming home intermittently to feed the baby, Bumby, because:

There were no baby-sitters then and Bumby would stay happy in his tall cage bed with his big, loving cat named F Puss. There were people who said it was dangerous to leave a cat with a baby. The most ignorant and prejudiced would say that a cat would suck a baby's breath and kill him. Others said that a cat would lie on a baby and the cat's weight would smother him. F Puss lay beside him in the tall cage bed and watched the door with his big yellow eyes, and would let no one come near him when we were out...

I can't attest to what Hemingway is attempting to evoke here, particularly regarding his contempt for the 'ignorant and prejudiced' who dared question the reliability of animal guardians. What I take from this passage is that Bumby was raised by a cat because it's very difficult to write stories or study the piano when you are caring for your child. Child care is a feminist issue, but moreover it is a capitalist issue and, like all capitalist issues, it is an issue for artists who, like (many, most?) women, are towards the bottom of the heap. Children might add value to one's life— intangible value, or at least nonquantifiable value— but they cost a lot, more than what some people possess. Having a baby will cost me money and time I do not have, and may never have, so the man I am in love with says he will have a vasectomy ($500) so that we will be able to learn to write side-by-side without leaving a young human in the care of domestic animals. (We have also ruled out pets, for now, and anything that leads to consumer debt.)

...

In London I felt a little bored. I was not particularly excited to go out consuming and not in the mood for art, either, sentiments which may be connected. So I took the bus to Oxford (£14 return) to see two friends: a couple, both young scholars but more than that—more golden, more like baubles singing. When I arrived, E was still polishing the references in the thesis she would submit the following morning, so to kill a few hours I walked around the old town. The sandstone everything of the ancient university was scorched—a sweaty brightness I did not enjoy—and so I ducked into Blackwell's, a large and famous but frankly quite boring bookshop. I couldn't find any of the books I was after, (*Unmastered: A Book on Desire, Most Difficult to Tell* by Katherine Angel, or *John Aubrey: My Own Life* by Ruth Scurr). But I dawdled nonetheless. Somewhere around the 'queer studies' section—a section comprised of four hundred copies of Maggie Nelson's *The Argonauts*, which I had read, already, twice, and little else—I found a stray copy of *I'm Very into You: Correspondence 1995–1996*, a collection of the emails Kathy Acker and McKenzie Wark sent one another after sleeping together when Acker visited Sydney in the mid-nineties.

A lush record of two minds, two hearts at work building lives for themselves that could seem vital, real. How much longing for recognition there is in their exchange, two queers living at the centre of things, or rather the centre of something marginal and vivid and alive, enmeshed in their times. Hemingway might paint a picture of what it is to be young, dumb, full of cum and choosing art over the affluence he'd inherit someday anyway, but he doesn't scratch the surface of the *how*, the *why*, the *superstructure*; he carries with him the security of Midwestern bourgeois prosperity. In 1995, Acker and Wark painted the grimness that seems much closer to my inheritance.

Acker:

> ...I'm this: part of a culture that doesn't want me...
> We're rats walking on tightropes we never thought
> existed. No medical insurance; no steady job; etc.
> This isn't me, Ken, or rather it is me (personal)
> and it isn't: it's social and political. All my friends
> are the same...Let me tell you about the America
> I live in. It's a war-zone. No wonder I'm fascinated
> with...by?...your relationships...we have the rela-
> tionships of too many rats in a cage.

Wark replies: 'There aren't enough vampires in this town. I mean hey, you've seen it. Here even the *artists* come to dinner and talk about real estate!'

Never mind that Acker, too, became free from work when her grandmother died, leaving her with close to a million dollars. Never mind that she had grown up in, and would always return to, the security of family money. Never mind that McKenzie Wark was able to professionalise her artistic work, because it was never far from being useful to an institution (the Australian government, universities). Never mind that most get to have neither.

The way I understand art in the arc of a life is similar to how I think about gender. In order to make art, really make it, the artist has to sacrifice the niceties. In order to comprehend that gender is hegemonic, we have to forgo the protections of patri-archy. One cannot kill all men and marry them for the status too. Or perhaps 'one' as a general subject can, but this particular one cannot, not in good faith. There is no getting around that. And yet. You want to be an artist because you want a little something of everything, but the having everything all at once prevents you from stepping back, from seeing the composition in high relief. The cliché—the artist outsider looking in—has to be true.

Acker was an outsider and she made a legend of herself. You could do that in San Francisco in the nineties, where there was 'a sign over the door...that [read] "straights not wanted here"'. She writes, 'I don't like prison gates in any form: they make me want to bust out. And I do. I want it all, you know?' I am guessing Acker wouldn't live in SF anymore—too expensive, all those plaid-clad tech bros—she'd live in Austin, or maybe Detroit, or, who knows, Minneapolis? Berlin. Athens. Is London possible still?

And Hemingway's hunger, albeit one that sustains itself from the axis of power: 'Standing there I wondered how much of what we had felt on the bridge was just hunger. I asked my wife and she said, "I don't know, Tatie. There are so many sorts of hunger...Memory is hunger."'

The niceties are culturally located. What is nice for me is not nice for you. Still, I like my luxury perfumes. Still, cheap produce makes me want to die. The hunger I have is bigger than any object. It is difficult to thoroughly imagine contentedness with some money or the love of a good man. Or with the soft drool of a dachshund. Or with even the reddest most mammalian orgasm. It is difficult to imagine being content for more than ten minutes with even the sharpest, creamiest parmesan crumbled over taut spaghetti, though this comes a little closer to it.

I have to employ my imagination to stabilise this idea. Content. Enough. *Satis.* An abstract condition. In place of the real thing or its semblance, my mind immediately makes the connection: to Satis House, the house where Miss Havisham and her ice-queen-in-training, her weapon against mankind, Estella, live. The association of that house and the thwarted lives trapped inside it sort of sums it up. Oh, irony. Oh, my days.

What would that feel like, *satis*? To put in a final day's work and dust yourself off. No. Acker, again: 'it's all boring and I want to work in this world and I want to matter.'

Friendship between Women

After a while you won't be able to turn on the Wim Wenders film *Paris, Texas* just because it is streaming on demand and it is Friday evening and you are living alone because he who has bale-coloured hair and sensitive skin is interstate working for the man. You won't be able to simply watch movies that too heavily idealise male loneliness or men's charming loserdom because you will be familiar with the concept by now, not that it wasn't once charming to you, you can still get around *Five Easy Pieces* starring Jack Nicholson, who was a star on the precipice, screaming for more of it, more of *life*, which some women found sexually attractive, not you, but you could relate to Jack Nicholson in the way that stars inspire false likeness by dramatising the fantasies ordinary people have of themselves, primarily the fantasy that one is proximate to the edge at all times. Susan Sontag said real celebrities don't play other characters they play themselves and they are coated with a sheen like velvet, forgive the misquote, who doesn't want to be coated in short tufted silk, warm somehow and dewy, like waking up when it's dark out still, turning on the bedside table lamp whose light traces on all skin and body types flatteringly; outside bed the morning is prickly and you reach across and envelop the hot form of him there there there velvet and there it is Jack Nicholson screaming.

Where are all the female Homer Simpsons a great woman once said. Look around baby you think to yourself look around there are female losers everywhere that's the point the point is you are drowning in female losers. Who wants to be Homer Simpson anyway when you could be Patty Bouvier anyway when did feminism get so up itself the point is that women too are stars of auteur films but auteur films are now plain life like women floundering with a sheen of volatility and velvet which some may find sexually attractive but with any luck it's plain life with a better functioning welfare state such that the Patty Bouviers of this world can mind themselves without having to go all I'm clawing my way out of this dump forthwith! Lisa Simpson's dogged righteousness was nonetheless another source of personal fantasy, the fantasy of discipline and conviction.

Many women you know are afraid of becoming old women who walk around glaring at the leaves on trees with one tit hanging out, if you add to this a natural predisposition for hard drinking or shadows or hard brows folding onto themselves, a distaste for the cult of excellence, there goes your chance of female prime ministership, whoosh. There was that woman you knew who said 'frankly' without adjusting her voice to indicate that she was aware that in this world 'frankly' is used only in ironic contexts, and no one despised her for it, frankly, she was steely nerved and got what she wanted thank you but did she also fear that animal inside her? The fantasy of the beast within that glint of it feral women share me too baby me too you were laughing just yesterday about that, you were always looking for females to not become but perhaps acquire females with a wolfish charisma like tangled hair and other such clichés and that's where you went wrong. When they did the beastly thing you dropped them like kittens in a dam lapping tiny tongues the slosh of it too cold at your ankles squatting over, you shoved them under and held tight come baby come sit on my lap you with your moral candour or so you would have them believe oh what big teeth you have clawing away from those girls forthwith.

I am writing about the time I broke up with a friend for her actions, a wolfish girl covered in sheen and volatility she behaved as nature had intended. I dropped her via email and she never emailed back.

The Literature
of Sadness

Look. I know you don't want to read about this, so I'll keep it brief. I'm sorry. But I met someone. Well, we had met before, but we re-met.

I re-met someone. Between meeting him years ago, in our home town, and then re-meeting him in Berlin years later, in the back of my mind I had entertained the thought that *maybe* this person was kind of a poser? Or that, *possibly*, the only towel he owned might smell like mould? Or I had pictured his subconscious, the other side of his face, and it was just a Meredith Music Festival tableau.

But I also thought: he's kind. I read his work and thought: he's talented. And then I saw him again, the first time we were both single, and I thought: oh. He's *beautiful*.

Now my only opinion of this man is that he is a fairy floss star cloud I want to float inside forever. I miss him when he's in the next room. I feel a buzz from his skin, radiant next to me when we lie down to read. I wake some nights in a hot love panic, squeezing his flesh like crazy. Lah lah lah. Like, flay me, lord. I've got it bad.

I told you. It's horrible. For two months, maybe three, I did nothing but cook elaborate meals and perform advanced sex moves and hide my cruel interpretations of other people's flawed personalities so that he would think I was the best. Best looking best read best fuck. I was supposed to be writing my thesis. Not googling 'love psychosis'. There's no *suspend time* button for when this happens. Friends expressed concern. Strangers in public gave unsolicited encouragement. Other things resolved themselves, as if by magic: things that had been asphyxiating me—the city I left, its lovelessness, my broke-ness and my overwork; family pains, my possessions, my fear of self-possession—all fell away. Calm took their place.

Kathy Acker hints at this transformative love power in *Blood and Guts in High School*:

> One of the most destructive forces in the world
> is love. For the following reason: The world is a
> conglomeration of objects, no, of events and the
> approachings of events towards objects, therefore
> of becoming stases static stagnant, of all that is
> unreal. You get in the world, you get your daily life

> your routine doesn't matter if you're rich poor legal
> illegal, you begin to believe what doesn't change
> is real, and love comes along and shows all these
> unchangeable forever fixtures to be flimsy paper
> bits. Love can tear anything to shreds.

Love shows us that the certainties we accept are arbitrary, flimsy paper bits. An entanglement of love-struck, horny auras interrupts the sense of urgency otherwise governing a person's existence in the world. *But*, while love is tearing everything to shreds, the 'unchangeable forever fixtures'—deadlines, rent, the obligation to call Mum and Dad—keep demanding some degree of participation. Love might reveal the true flakiness of ideology, but adhering to it—participating in reality—is what keeps the heating bill paid. In those first few months, in love with him, I couldn't work—not in the way I had been in the habit of working. The fruitlessness and masochism of that kind of toil was too hard to bear. So, during this love binge I performed only the bare minimum of labour: a column, an essay that was overdue, a book review I had agreed to months before, revisions on a paper. No new objects passed through my hands. I couldn't bring myself to start any writing that might expand my little world.

This could happen to you. And when it does, you'll find yourself gravitating towards the grimmest specimens of culture for entertainment. Why? Self-punishment for your rapture. Or, an inverted sense of cruelty. Or, a twisted sense of social duty: my private joy does not erase history's endless inhumanity.

Or is it simpler than that? Aside from the initial shock of familiarity you find in love, a new relationship is small. It is time slowing down so you can learn the precise tininess of your lover's world—the other's world—while matter and moments forge onwards. When things are going well in your puny, daily island life, the macro-drama, the *real* action, is happening offstage, elsewhere. So you read (or watch films or listen to music) to keep a foot in it; high drama, crushing injustice. Absolute misery. Trump.

Why is it that the closer we get to sadness the realer we feel?

Sadness is the glue between the days as we live in them. Sadness is the other face of those object-events, the face of the world that stagnates and abnegates and doesn't much change. By 'sadness' I don't mean depression; I don't mean the feeling of *poor, pathetic me*. I mean the bodily response when humour, and life, have been extinguished. The opposite of love. The closing down of possibility—and the reluctance to see and name and claim possibility when it appears. Self-hatred. Emotional ineptitude. Complicity. Complacency. Overwhelming meh-ness.

Not long into our rapture I got an email advertising a Verso Books online sale, fifty per cent off. We scrolled through the catalogue of intellectual ambition and purchased what ended up being two blue plastic sacks' worth of radical books, all for fifty or sixty Australian dollars. This is something you do when you are suddenly in love: you purchase the aspiration to understand the true horror that hegemony entails (theoretically, at least). You think: *Adorno never let his heart turn to mush, and nor will I!* You think: *now that I am in love I am ready to face it all, with strength and with courage. I am ready now!* You think: *is love a terribly bourgeois conceit?* You think: *will our necks be first on the butcher's block?*

When the books arrived a few weeks later, the days were already winter-dark. I took a photo of my lover in his tracksuit, holding the Verso sacks at his sides like a radical Santa, and posted it on Instagram. Waited for the meagre stream of likes to arrive, from the few of my social media 'friends' who remained tolerant of my reports on the State of My Love for Him (Critical).

Did I read all those books on the powers of mourning and radical sexual futures and anti-colonial pedagogies? No. Though I skim-read a few chapters. Thank heavens that one of the books we bought was a graphic narrative. Basically a comic. Readable in one short sitting and with some pleasure. After finishing *Red Rosa*, Kate Evans's graphic biography of Rosa Luxemburg, I sat on the edge of my bed and wept. *Rosa Luxemburg was murdered!* How could anyone be expected to bear the sadness of that? Of course, I had known she was murdered—the day I read the book was the ninety-eighth anniversary of her death, and a commemorative march, held two kilometres from my apartment, passed by the spot where the paramilitaries threw her corpse into the canal. She was murdered, and *Red Rosa* addresses this fact with the fullness of its tragedy. She was murdered, and if she hadn't been murdered, things might have gone differently. Germany as the (possible, imagined) socialist republic might not have become Nazi Germany.

Then again, if Luxemburg hadn't been murdered in 1919, she'd have been murdered in 1920.

Luxemburg's death was no secret—not at all—though there was some mystery shrouding her remains, which were only recovered in 2009. Assassinations like Luxemburg's were cease-and-desist warnings to—in this case—revolutionary socialists;

they were done with the express intention of inciting terror. Of shutting people up. Normalising the sadness, the despair, of forced complicity.

For the first time in my reading life, there are radical, political, even (at a stretch) revolutionary books on recommended reading lists in mainstream magazines and on bestseller and prize lists—what's beautiful and cool can now be politically 'worthy', too. But the term 'political literature' still leads to eye-rolls. It conjures up images of working-class white families, or refugees not from vast metropolises, or sad queers, suffering as they ought to: in ugly clothes. These people don't laugh, don't joke around, don't secretly believe they are the devastating stars of the melodrama of their lives—they stoically plod through their misery and mud. 'Political writing', as opposed to political *reading*—which sees every book as a site of potential political meaning and imagining—is still laden by association with a gritty kind of Marxist realism. This idea, that the normative domain of 'politics' is just suffering without style (or humour), comes, I suspect, from the notion that exposing 'the truth' of injustice will go some way to correcting it. And that the truth will be immediately discernible: it will be the ugliest thing; the thing we most want to turn away from. As though the individuals who make up a society are only complicit in any given injustice because 'the truth' has been hidden from them. As though people eat meat only because they don't know about factory farming; they use iPhones only because they don't know about the suicides at Foxconn; they accept a government's forced internment of migrants at the near-end of perilous journeys only because they don't know what the inside of a prison looks like. This might be what critic Paul Stephens names 'the information dialectic', the idea that 'greater access to information does not necessarily lead to increasing enlightenment'.

This era is one of endlessly proliferating images. If you haven't seen an image of the terrible thing, it's because you don't want to. As Roland Barthes writes, 'no photograph has ever convinced or refuted anyone'. He says that the signified, the denoted (the real-life analogue that an image, a text, ostensibly portrays), the—for example—fact that Rosa Luxemburg was murdered, is not itself sufficiently meaningful. It's in the signifier, the connotation (what 'society' thinks about something), the—for example—fact that Luxemburg was powerless against Nazi thugs and died for it, that a more potent truth is uncovered.

But the denoted—the real-life flesh facts—are never neutral, entirely, not insofar as they are *always* understood through the culturally mediated field of language. The 'culture' changes over time due to the changing nature of which truths—which images and texts; which narratives—best serve and preserve a given society's peace of mind. What happens when those images, the true, ugly ones, are exposed? Maggie Nelson writes:

> ...'knowing the truth' does not come with redemption as a guarantee, nor does a feeling of redemption guarantee an end to a cycle of wrongdoing. Some would even say it is key to maintaining it, insofar as it can work as a reset button—a purge that cleans the slate, without any guarantee of change at the root.

The gruesome images that are now part of our visual vocabulary, of Abu Ghraib victims, or of Eric Garner's murder, work simultaneously to expose certain violent realities to the hard-to-convince (those with a stake in 'not knowing'); to abrade old wounds; to allow some to shirk their complicity (*a dangerous cop, a gang of cruel soldiers; not my kind, not* me); and also, crucially, to advance the legal standing of victims. A tool of justice, a weapon of torture, an evasion. A graphic reminder of something you know too well, or something you'd rather not know.

So why attempt to understand 'politics'—the mechanics of power and oppression—through the sliding, unsatisfying prism of the ugly truth? Why not, instead, read politics as it is mediated through fiction, poetry, or the artifice of life writing? At a remove, at an interpretive distance?

Although *Red Rosa* is mostly grounded in fact, its diversions from historical accuracy (which are meticulously noted at the book's end) permit it to enter a liminal state. The possibilities that fiction presents allow *Red Rosa* to be moving, theme-y, sad and, above all, idealistic. It allows one version of reality to be contained by the manageable parameters of literature.

One of *Red Rosa*'s sweetest pleasures is its incorporation of some of Luxemburg's personal writings, also collected in another Verso title, *The Complete Works of Rosa Luxemburg*, where she delights in being alive, in being a body in the world. From prison, she writes to her lover: 'The hour before sunset has a magic all its own. The sun was still hot, but one gladly allowed its slanted rays to burn on one's neck and cheeks like a kiss.'

Politics is not removed from the way the sun kisses your neck at the hour before sunset. Politics is the pleasure in the body and the imagination, too.

...

Other books I read during my love panic: *The Notebook*, *The Proof* and *The Third Lie* are, together, a trilogy by the Hungarian-born, Swiss-émigré author Ágota Kristóf. Some of the saddest novels I have ever read. They take place in and around a Hungarian village during some key events of the twentieth century: World War II consumes the village, which has a transit camp at its periphery; the Communists take over and torture their prisoners; then, a quiet nationalist revolution occurs, a change of power yet again.

None of these events are named outright. In an interview, Kristóf said that she 'did not want to name anything'. But one needn't be told which of the trilogy's officers are Nazis (the ones with caviar dripping from their lips), which are Russians (the ones gang-raping everything that moves), which civilians are Jews (the ones who appear for a moment and then are gone forever). The first novel in the trilogy is written in the spare language of its two child narrators, the 'we' of twins Claus and Lucas. *The Notebook* is the notebook in which they record 'everything that happens' to them during these tumultuous years. The violence of wartime and political precarity is laid bare, but it is in interpersonal politics that we see the grave effects of war; for example, almost every child we encounter is subjected to some form of sexual molestation. In a different interview, Kristóf said that 'during the war, there are a lot fewer secrets, rape is freed', and these novels clearly describe this unsettling wartime moral ambiguity. But in the moral landscape of Kristóf's grim world, trauma is not predictable or clean. In this regard, these novels comprise a rich psychoanalytic tapestry; characters do not always act in line with their interests, and their traumas are not exactly what we might expect them to be. Scenes of rape and other forms of molestation are tangled up with a childhood obsession with sex. And the twins' moral landscape is itself stark: they feed a soldier who has defected because he 'absolutely needs' to eat; they blow gunpowder up in the face of a friend because she has been cruel to a procession of Jews being 'deported'.

The Proof and *The Third Lie* help make sense of *The Notebook* in metafictional terms. As the narrative develops across the three novels, each storyline the reader is ingratiated into is later pulled from under her feet; every one of them is called into question—fiction within fiction, time outside time? Yet it doesn't seem that this narrative corruption is for the purpose of delivering a 'clever' comment on fiction and reality. Instead it seems to be saying something about the relationship between mortal solitude and writing.

In *The Third Lie*, Lucas is asked what he is writing:

> I answer that I try to write true stories but that at a given point the story becomes unbearable because of its very truth, and then I have to change it. I tell her I try to tell my story but all of a sudden I can't—I don't have the courage, it hurts too much. And so I embellish everything and describe things not as they happened but the way I wish they had happened.

In another of Kristóf's few translated interviews, she states that her novels are more or less autobiographical. When the interviewer asks Kristóf about certain elements of her fiction, she responds with claims like: 'It is more or less a true story.' Her insistence on this neat parallel between life and fiction betrays the radical transformation that occurs when information passes between these two domains—but so too does it hint at their interdependence. Lucas says: 'No book, no matter how sad, can be as sad as a life.' It is the writing *within* a life that gives moments of reprieve from solitude.

These novels were not written to 'speak truth to power'. What would be the point of speaking truth to power when your days are long and cold and loveless? 'Laying it bare' doesn't go far enough, either. But this trilogy is nonetheless political, in that it shows us that the rootlessness and isolation brought about by the tides of history can be unbearable to live through. The telling of such a tale does not hope to expose 'the truth' and then circumvent its injustices; instead it shows us a world where the things that happen in a life, all the terrible things and the joyful things too, can exist in a neatly comprehensible form—a novel— which can be contained on paper pages, and bound, and held in a hand, and passed between people, and consequently, unlike real life, *managed*.

On the opening page of another very sad book I read while falling into blissful love, *A Sorrow Beyond Dreams* by Peter Handke, the author says: 'My mother has been dead for almost seven weeks; I had better get to work before the need to write about her, which I had felt so strongly at her funeral, dies away and I fall back into the dull speechlessness with which I reacted to the news of her suicide.'

My lover said to me, possibly to impress me with his sensitivity to gender norms, 'What a *masculine* opening.' And he might be right: this urge to capture a feeling before it slips away into 'dull speechlessness' demonstrates the violent ordering, the formal enslavement that is writing, and reminds me that writing is the kind of occupation that thrives in cultures that are built upon accumulation. And yet, it's a masculine gesture I feel comfortable identifying with. I need to manage the unmanageable, to contain, correct and formalise the world, because I need to survive it.

A Sorrow Beyond Dreams is an essay-length biographical portrait of the author's recently suicided mother. It examines her life from beginning to sorrowful end, grappling with the senselessness of her wasted potential. Her life was marked by not-having: not pleasure, not education, not voice, not freedom, not choice. Self-administered abortions. Injuries from one violent man or another. Illness. Pain.

If Kristóf's trilogy creates the possibility of a parallel literary universe where the germ of moral courage can infect the imagination, Handke's view of things is much bleaker. Upon hearing of his mother's suicide, Handke finds that suddenly 'my day-to-day world—which, after all, consists only of images repeated *ad nauseum* over a period of years and decades since they were new—fell apart, and my mind became so empty it ached'. In his misery, all of life becomes simply an endless repetition of banal moments. Acker's unchangeable forever fixtures. The mechanics of sadness.

The tragedy of Handke's mother's life is not unique. It is the life of untold women and men from nowhere, who have no power, not even over the course of their daily lives. In trying to describe this sadness that is the world, Handke touches on the corollary of his urge to 'capture' with writing that which would otherwise slip away: that despite its promise to make the unmanageable manageable, language is not a complete tool for recording the world. He writes, 'In stories we often read that something or other is "unnameable" or "indescribable"; ordinarily this strikes me as a cheap excuse. This story, however, is really about the nameless, about speechless moments of terror.' Towards the end of the essay, Handke states that in the act of writing he has failed to alleviate terror and enormous grief:

> Obviously narration is only an act of memory; on the other hand, it holds nothing in reserve for future use; it merely derives a little pleasure from states of dread by trying to formulate them as aptly as possible; from enjoyment of horror it produces enjoyment of memory.

Which leads me to ask if this is what writing is. Writing is the collision of thoughts with events, translated into a material form and then back again into the whisper of a feeling. But when the action is happening elsewhere—for example, when your world is puny because you are in love—perhaps the *writing* is happening elsewhere. The writing is the urgency to translate and contain what is happening, when what is happening demands to be contained.

Instead of talking about 'political literature'—because the term is outdated, because it doesn't adequately describe the literature that makes us feel the most 'in the world' and the best prepared to reject the intolerable—why not talk about the *literature of sadness*. If love tears everything to shreds, sad books, like sadness itself, demonstrate that the unchangeable forever fixtures are the same things that kill us. We wish to be redeemed from this muddy truth, but we won't be. Did Rosa Luxemburg get to escape her assassination just by knowing it was coming?

. . .

Apart from this temporary love-blessed reprieve, in general I am not a 'happy' person. In general, I unreasonably assume I am difficult and unlikeable. I assume that every email contains a threat. I am genuinely surprised when people don't torture their children or animals. When I am in the habit of writing every day, sometimes it feels that I am writing because writing is trying not to die. Or writing is trying not to become a hopeless alcoholic. This sounds melodramatic, for sure, and I say it only to suggest that sadness is not always a terrible illness. Sadness is, perhaps, the most honest response to living.

Turning Thirty

○ How did I get to thirty without knowing how to trim the
  length of a screw?

> \+ Don't know if 'trim' is the correct word here or
>   even 'screw'. (Quietly, I'm proud that I know the
>   word for 'thread', the ribbed valley circling the
>   screw-like object.)

○ How did I experience an entire twenties without several
  doomed and haunting love affairs? I mean, all my
  relationships failed, except for this one I'm in right now,
  and most of them failed miserably. But their failures were
  not at all poetical.

+ The older I get, the less doomed I feel. I'm pleased about that. Though this fix is a trick.

> – *Every extra day increases the chance of full-scale disaster.*

> – Or each new day the chances are just the same as always.

○ How did I get here without first learning to wear pastels?

○ Or be thin?

> + I think, *I should have spent the past ten years learning how to tolerate exercise.*

> + And then I think, *What's so fucking good about pilates?*

> > – What did *getting on your knees to disappear* ever get anyone?

○ Some people believe in nothing. Not no thing, but *nothing*. Not me.

○ I watched the miniseries *Angels in America* recently, all of it. In the first episode, I cried my heart out. Beautiful, good, gorgeous men, falling into nothing.

> + Then I got bored of the whole New York-y aspirational upper-class vibe. The final scene, where the four now-friends—Belize the regal nurse, Prior the survivor, Louis the over-thinker and Hannah the ex-Mormon—sit in the shadow of the Angel of the Waters in Central Park,

discussing the Gorbachev-y, 'settlements'-y news of 1990. They all have these chatty, flirty *opinions*.

+ I rolled my eyes. It was all so *average*. But I watched it till the credits played out.

    – I rolled my eyes because frivolity mixed with the fruits of abundance (decadence) is the easiest thing to eye-roll at. But the truth is that its opposite is even worse.

    – I rolled my eyes because so many of my desires were structured around the aesthetics of this New York-y aspirational upper-class thing, which suddenly disappointed me. My gutlessness, my naivety.

○ My apartment is now ninety-five per cent finished. Ninety-five per cent is the percentage of finished that, once reached, might never be surpassed. I painted the bathroom's tiled floor black, but we needed to use the bathroom, so I didn't get any further. It still needs one more coat. Will I get on my knees this weekend and actually paint it? I hope so. I really do.

    + Half-finished home renovations recall a mode of living I was for most of my life comfortable with, but which in recent years I've been trying to abolish. Things like half-painted walls which remain half-painted forever I used to not notice and now they tip me over the edge.

○ When I was little, sitting in the back of the car, I'd frown at houses I deemed 'ugly', as though they were committing an act of hostility against me. I'd smile, however, at the posh houses.

○ My family's house then wasn't a 'nice' house, but we had an overgrown front yard, which was charming. And we had guinea pigs, a dog, a cat and chickens, and for one minute, a pony, which other children envied.

  + We next lived in a small town in the country, where the appearance of houses was important.

  + A classmate described my house as a *shanty house*, which was both politically incorrect and untrue, but which wounded my pride.

    – Wounded the foundations of my house-pride.

  + The town's menacing *Better Homes and Gardens* atmosphere unsettled my parents, who hadn't come from there, and we left. By this time, Sydney, where we had come from, was a rich person's city. So the industrial scrub of Melbourne's north it was.

  + I was very excited to meet my new 'Melbourne' friends, who would be highly cerebral tween punks.

    – The only punks I found were highly cerebral stoners, which is to say they loved impersonating Cartman.

◦ In my first week in Melbourne I put a pair of eight-hole cherry Docs on lay-by.

◦ In my first month, I became a baby recruit to a socialist party. I went to revolution-planning meetings every Saturday. I couldn't honestly see myself storming parliament in ugly fatigues, but in principle the socialists were okay. Besides, I had no friends other than the friend I cajoled into coming to meetings with me, so it was, at least, something to do. I read Karl Marx (slowly) and sold radical newspapers in my school uniform at Flinders Street Station (boldly). But if I'm honest I was always a dilettante about these things.

　　+ One night I went to some sort of afterparty the socialists were throwing at one of their houses. The place was an open-plan, newly renovated apartment on Swanston Street. The guy who lived there was seventeen or eighteen.

　　　　– Don't trust a socialist who's never held down a degrading job.

◦ My mother thought I had been tricked by some alluring older man into joining this cult, but that's only because she'd never met a socialist male from the early noughts. Their facial hair was *atrocious*.

◦ The socialists all smoked cigarettes, but none of them ever ate McDonald's. There was, I suppose, an unspoken distinction between these filthy habits. I worked at, and often ate, McDonald's, but didn't mention it.

○ Which is not to say I learned nothing.

+ I learned that all the sexist slurs I used on the regular were in fact *sexist slurs*, part of a larger project of degrading women. This transformed me.

+ I learned that there are people who believe a revolution can be bloodless.

+ I learned the words for my political outrage, about the legacy of people saying no.

+ I learned that men with unkempt beards and a theoretical understanding of the patriarchy don't ask you questions if you're a young girl.

- Years later, I learned they don't start asking you questions when you're grown, either.

+ Anyway, I couldn't afford the dues.

○ I keep getting these flashbacks.

+ Like what people say happens in their seventies, eighties.

+ Thirty's not so old. But it's not young, either.

+ It's all just so sharp and clear now.

○ A few months ago, I bought an apartment. Well, I split the cost with my boyfriend, who is actually now my husband. So I'm turning thirty as a married homeowner, which is definitely not how I thought things would go.

+ Our apartment is in a place where we won't be able to find work, so we've agreed to periodically come back to Melbourne and save like demons in order to live in our place.

+ That will mean living skint in both cities, which is fine by me.

+ Living skint is not so easy in Melbourne, though, not these days. People there spend a lot of time convincing you they are very poor, and then they wash their dishes with Aesop hand gel.

> – It's probably not called 'hand gel'.
> Hand-cleaning fluid. Palm wash.
> Finger clean. *Savon pour les extrémités*.
> Soap?

o Other things happen. In the world and inside the home and body. When a person turns thirty.

+ Today was the forty-fourth anniversary of the Athens Polytechnic uprising that is credited with bringing down the military junta in Greece. The rain this morning stifled the early-morning protests, but later in the arvo we went down to the main rally. It was moving and fearsome. There must have been at least twenty thousand people.

> – A few hundred young revolutionaries in the front line linked arms, and each of them held a red flag attached to a

broomstick in one fist and a motorcycle
helmet in the other.

- The riot police mirrored them, but with
a cartoonish glint of horror. An identical
line, but this one with military haircuts
and firearms.

- The chanting was deep, unified.
Like church.

- The air was tense and I felt afraid.
And proud. And pissed off.

- There was only one woman in the
front line.

+ Yesterday, at least sixteen people were killed
in flash floods on the outskirts of Athens. Photos
show red mud rivers that used to be streets,
upturned cars. People whose houses had filled
with water a metre deep. *I'm wearing sandals*,
said an older man on the news, *because they're
all I have now.*

+ Just now, I went outside to pull the old cane
chairs off the balcony before they got destroyed—
it's hailing and raining at the same time—and I
took in a big breath of the livid air. It smelled like
a chemical fire. There's been so much lightning
the smell could be from a fire.

+ Eleven days ago, a few guys on motorcycles shot
  at a van parked outside the socialist party's headquarters, half a kilometre from our place. Yesterday,
  an anarchist group took responsibility for it. Part of
  their 17 November insurrection.

+ Last night, walking around, I saw that most of
  the stores were closed and shuttered. In solidarity?
  Or to secure themselves against property damage?
  The things you don't know when you're new
  in town.

+ Yesterday, the IMF conceded that they had got
  the bailout wrong, that the austerity package may
  have been a bad idea. As in: they didn't anticipate
  the extent of the recession that ensued.

    – Right.

+ Earlier, before going out to get a pie, Dom and
  I had sex in the kitchen. It was great. The cabinet
  in our new kitchen is the perfect height, which is
  good to know.

+ Tonight, we will have dinner with a self-identified
  anarchist who will tell me that 'identitarian' politics
  is destroying the 'workers movement'.

        – I will tell him that if the first thing
          he hears when he hears the words
          'feminism' or 'queer' or 'Black
          liberation' is that he's *not invited*,

then he is probably not all that invested in redistributing power sideways.

– He'll explain to me slowly and without pause the reasoning behind his position, as if Twitter had never been invented.

– I'll get a major cramp in my gut, think it's food poisoning and go home before anyone has even finished their meal. By the time I'm in bed, the cramping will be gone completely.

+ Tomorrow, I'll wake up early and read for an hour or two before getting up. Because I'm not scared of time running away from me now. Then I'll make coffee and do whatever dishes there are and wipe all the surfaces before starting work.

∘ Me, wishing domestic concerns had no impact on the day's productivity.

∘ Me, secretly delighting in becoming a crappy kind of homemaker.

+ But nothing's a choice, though, is it? It was waiting for me all along.

∘ None of the cabinets in the apartment have door knobs yet—I bought a box of them, they arrived the other day, but the screws are all the wrong lengths and I don't know how to trim them, or even what tool I will need. This is probably the most bourgeois problem I've ever had.

But I'm not bourgeois enough (yet?) to hire a person to work it out for me. And I don't know handy people. Not here. So if I want to open a cupboard, I have to squat down and press my fingertips up hard on the edge of the door and pull it towards me.

+ This is more difficult than it probably sounds.

○ Things have slowed down and at the same time they have sped up. The cord part of my phone charger broke a few days ago and I haven't bought a new one. I might get another one soon, but also I might not. Because I don't really need a phone right now.

+ Thirty is old enough to realise the link between looking at other people's photos of their fantasy lives and feeling fraught, fat and misinformed.

○ I don't want as much now as I used to want.

+ I always longed for these hideous guttings, leaks of anguished, bloody love. And to wake up alone and unscathed. For my work to be anointed by the blessings of the someones higher up.

– Not anymore.

+ Now I want an emotional range of five to eight. Nothing less than *average*. But nothing more than *surprisingly good*.

+ I have more now than I ever did before. Or maybe now I know it.

Houses

Behind the serene vases of flowers, behind the teapots,
the rugs and the waxed floors, is the other, the true face
of the house, the horrible face of the crumbled house.
— Natalia Ginzburg, 'The Son of Man'

The city without love is an unjust and cruel city.
— Elena Ferrante, *Frantumaglia*

In the twenty-second house one night, it's an apartment, really,
you make me spanakopita. We agree that the spinach in Germany
is okay, not limp and tasteless like the other supermarket vege-
tables here, and we wash it down with a three-euro bottle of
bordeaux. We eat so early here, it's disconcerting. The light drops
out quickly at the four p.m. dusk—a smashed rose petal one
second, blue-black the next—and the almost-always darkness
of this city is almost-always suggestive of mild depression, or of
moody love. From our narrow kitchen table, I look across the
courtyard into other people's yellow windows. For the first time
in forever, I'm in love, and so, for a moment, I see every other
couple in the world finishing their meals together, delaying bed

with a bottle of something, while at the same time I feel that we have invented a new tradition. Called eating dinner together.

We pack up the dishes and enter the warm burrow of darkness. The bedroom is the only room we keep heated with the old Berlin pipe heaters.

...

I don't know whether to put in the things I do not remember as well as the things I do remember.

...

The way we lived—my family, that is, in childhood—was that Mum, Dad, my brothers and I shared a house. It shifted place and shape a few times, but it remained steadfast in its spiritual arrangement, which was more or less a rejection of the petty tyranny of the domestic. This manifested as a bohemian chaos that my friends feared and pitied, and that their parents, at least some of them, looked upon smilingly. Bedlam permeated the gaps between every object, the result of working, breathing life. But it would be careless to dismiss the moral superiority, the presumed nobility, of that mess. Grubbiness, in suburban life, can speak to the spirit that soars above the corporeal. If there's not enough money for self-determination, at least you can have Charlie Parker playing in a room full of people who are screaming 'where *is* my shoe/homework/cat'. Something honourable about that. A family of opinionated men (even the females in our house were male) rejects beauteous domestic order as uptight, prissy and superficial. While every once in a while we'd have to 'blitz' the house—bundle up the rank laundry, hose down the dying shrubbery, powder every floor with lavender-scented carpet deodoriser and suck it up again with the vacuum—the idea that a space could be controlled by human discipline appeared never to cross my parents' minds.

A little boy who lived down the street, who was eventually forbidden to play with my brothers and me, had, in his house, a perfectly white room. His father was an air traffic controller and slept all day. His mother guarded the silence fiercely. These facts, the dewy weight of clouds, the starched pilot's uniform, the white colour of sleep, have congealed in my memory of this room, this living room that was governed by the principle of sleep. It was no coincidence that children were prohibited from entering.

My mother lit up with laughter when we reported to her this strange room. Cold, she'd say to describe people like that. Mean. Stingy.

...

In the twenty-second house, I dangle your underwear from a priggish finger. This classical pose says, Could you *please* pick up after yourself. It says, Do you *see* me here at *all*?

It says, I long to live with you in a perfectly white room.

White rabbit-fleece carpet; a wide bed piled high with down, silk, velvet; a bright marble desk. Dead silence, and the whisper of a fingernail sliding over the page. The buoyant fragrance of narcissus.

A windowless monad? I have declined the nobility of mess, wanting instead to live untouched by others. As though this childhood, emancipated from the hegemony of order, had no emancipatory effect on me at all.

...

Australians are passionate about property. I got that line off the internet, from the real-estate website Domain dot com, but it could have come from anyone's mouth. We Australians are passionate about property.

...

You and I sit together looking at apartments in Athens online, eighteen thousand euro for a studio, fifty thousand for a two-bedroom in a down-and-out area. Being from Melbourne we know that down-and-out areas yield high returns in the long term, but perhaps we don't know a thing about Europe, its history of forever down-and-outedness. You and I are flirting with property. Together we have pooled some money I have saved from my scholarship, from teaching and waitressing, you your prize money and a bump up from your grandmother's will. And then; although I believe I can commit to you and I can commit to living long enough to pay the price of a passion for property, the idea of permanency, or a longer-than-two-year residency, fills me with terror.

...

The third house, *home*, maybe, was white double-fronted weatherboard with colonial green trim, then after a renovation frenzy heritage cream with colonial green trim and a colonial green Colorbond roof. A lot of colonialism for a cheap cottage built sometime during the post-war decades to accommodate the nobodies coming back from war, the nobodies coming from other countries, not knowing there'd be no garlic here, nor parsley.

An elm so old it reached out halfway across the backyard. We called it an elm, but it was in fact a box elder maple. A quarter acre; chickens down the back; an ancient apple tree, diseased, with black-barnacled fruit. We installed the Hills hoist, added the fibro extension. Rose, the previous tenant of this quarter acre, was briefly, famously, the oldest person in town. Did we visit her before she died? Was she a hundred and nine?

...

The fifth house is the other home. Home Number Two. Home in this case is not a warm feeling but one of desolation. It's been years since I lived there, yet still I dream about it with a dread that cannot be argued into good-sport spirits. A sullen and deprived teenager feeling. Brick cladding, and sinking into silt, the fifth house had no right angles; its doors were constantly ajar. The view from the lounge-room window was of a street lined with panel beaters. The sky above it was pugnaciously grey. After a decade or more there, my parents passed this house along to some person more passionate about home renovations than they ever were. Some keen bean in the property market. Then they moved into a rental near the station for five years, and then, now, to their final (or so they say) house, a brick thing with tall, wide windows at the furthest edge of the city. Dad finally retired, Mum will work forever, and the two of them have taken up an interest in indigenous botany. The garden they are building there is lovely.

...

After leaving my parents' house at eighteen, I count sixteen moves, but possibly there were more. If you want to contact me, email or skype. Or just don't. Old-fashioned mail is (usually) out of the question.

Through my frequent use of iPhone apps, my movements are recorded and stored for private trade between corporations I have never heard of. This is not as…romantic? to me now as it might once have sounded. For example, I ordered a yearly planner online. To place the order, I was asked to enter all my personal data—birth date, sex, things that would seem irrelevant unless I was booking in for surgery. I ticked the terms and conditions box, of course, which presumably outlined all the ways in which this online store planned to sell my personal information. Normally, faced with such an invasion of privacy, I'd close my laptop, put on a broad-brimmed hat and tram it to a bookstore. But now is not *normally*—I'm staying temporarily in a city I don't belong to, which doesn't sell the planner I want in the language I speak. It's cold outside. Freezing. These small desires for small comforts left unmet accumulate in a mundane sort of way. Nothing much happens with them; they just accrue to create a sense of incompleteness.

Partly, I am in a city I don't belong to because it is affordable, and I can work from home, from anywhere. Partly, I am here because I can be. Because I have let myself remain untethered, as frivolous a privilege as it is perilous. Partly, too, I am in a city I haven't been invited to because melancholy elsewhere is more bearable than melancholy at home.

In her book *Traumascapes*, Maria Tumarkin writes about her wish to avoid tourist activities at all costs when she's abroad. *Tourist*, she writes,

> is a category from which I obsessively exclude
> myself. My inner need to have a different kind

of presence is overwhelming. I buy no souvenirs, walk purposefully, eat and drink little and try to avoid, if I can, obvious landmarks and destinations...In other words, I try to enjoy myself as little as possible.

Until I read that passage, I didn't know it was possible to excise oneself from the category. When I leave Australia it's rarely because of an enduring need I have to see the landmarks deemed historical by government men or guidebooks. More likely I am fleeing, for a moment, what I see as the oppressive small-mindedness of my people.

It does not escape me that when I set foot in a city that is new to me, I am likely to encounter minds just as small, and just as oppressive, as those I am escaping, or my own. All people must live their daily lives, and to live a daily life is to live a narrow life. But the people in these places, 'other' places, places other than *my* place, crucially, are not *my* small-minded people—I wasn't raised within their institutions, I don't know the cruellest terms in their dialects—and so for a few weeks, a month, or more, I'm suspended from the burden of seeing reflected my own petty cruelties in the day-to-day world around me.

Which is precisely what makes me a tourist, if I use Jamaica Kincaid's thinking. Her description of the asymmetry of power in an encounter between the 'native' and the tourist:

> ...some natives—most natives in the world—cannot go anywhere. They are too poor...They are too poor to escape the reality of their lives; and they are too poor to live properly in the place where they live, which is the very place you, the tourist,

want to go—so when the natives see you, the tourist, they envy you, they envy your ability to leave your own banality and boredom, they envy your ability to turn their own banality and boredom into a source of pleasure for yourself.

...

At an age when I didn't know that I could do as I liked, that I could choose to remain untethered, that I could disappoint my parents or anyone else and it wouldn't affect the spinning of the globe, I went overseas (on credit—barely legal), a gambling-dad kind of move, wildly irresponsible, but once there, *overseas!*, for the first time, I felt compelled to tick off the main attractions. I was never really sure what I was looking at, or why. When I arrived in Newcastle, English Newcastle, to meet Dad's family for the first time, a sweet cousin my age I'd never met before picked me up. He drove me home the long way, awkwardly pointing out an obelisk at the axis of the roundabout we circled. Because his mother had suggested he do so. I felt ignorant for not knowing what it was I was supposed to see.

In Paris—mecca of clueless tourism: cathedral, bridge, tower—I visited Oscar Wilde's tomb at Père Lachaise, its elegant masonry eroding beneath layers of fetid lipstick. At the crypt, I waited. For something to click in me. I don't think I expected to feel moved, exactly, but I wasn't prepared for the *nothing* I felt in my heart. I didn't leave greasy lip marks of my own, even though I had just read and adored *Dorian Gray*. I sat on a bench and wrote in my diary, a diary I was rigorously filling with untruths, preparing for the horror of somebody reading how desperate my day-to-day had become. Although I was *overseas!* I was still a sad teenage girl: my heart was torn up, I didn't know how I was going to pay off my rapidly increasing credit-card debt, I was paralysed by the truth of my not being any of the people I longed to be. I wasn't grown enough to untangle my desires from my reality. If being grown is desirable at all. My writing, even my diary writing, was terrible. Not because I didn't know about sentences, or because I didn't have literary ambitions, but because I couldn't tell a truth. Insincerity, I now know, is the language of those who deny their interiority. Sitting in Père Lachaise that spring afternoon, I scribbled false feelings I'd had about Jim Morrison, wilted flowers, ancient death all around. A tourist. A bore. Nothing more.

...

The seventh house, down a mediaeval alley in central Barcelona, was formerly a flamenco bar. A squat, really. In this dwelling, my new friend Annalisa posed the topic for the afternoon's discussion: *With liberty there's no justice; with justice there's no liberty.* A college application essay question she'd recently aced. We rolled up the overhead door that separated my garage-bedroom from the sulphur stench of the street, pulled the tatty couch to the edge where the house met the *plaça* and drank innocent tea in the sun.

The question posed a serious problem for me. I wanted justice and I wanted liberty and I didn't want to choose.

It was summer, and the speed fiends from Italy had come over to Barcelona and taken up residence in the square my place backed onto. They had come across the sea because, they told us, the drugs were more plentiful in Spain that year, and sleeping rough was safer. These men and women, whose every cell depended on chemical gratification, struck me as vivid shadows: they'd slip between rage and affection, terrible agony and glorious elation. Like us. But more. But more.

As the blistering heat drew on, a woman who slept curled up in a rug in a private corner of the *plaça*, wild curls on her head, became more and more primitive. Seeing her terrible freedom—in the clutches of dependence—I felt that I could very easily become her. That I was forever on the cusp of being her, and that this was not an identification I was supposed to feel. She stalked the alleyways with her chest completely bare. She held her emotions like trophies. From my window, I saw a man charge his flesh into her, for cash, or maybe for something harder. I looked away and then looked back. I thought about all the women I knew and didn't know who compelled me, who I revolved around as though they were the sun. Women who were looking for something other than a home. Looking, maybe, for something harder. Would do terrible things to get it. The city's smell, a complex funk from the bowels of ancient plumbing, I grew to associate with *liberty*, deep and rattling. Terror dark red *freedom*, and not, not ever, justice.

Everything then was rich with abundance. And everywhere was true danger.

...

At the age of seventeen, Jamaica Kincaid was sent from her native Antigua to New York City to work as a domestic servant to earn money for her family. Once there, she decided to cease her remittance payments to her mother. They had had a difficult relationship. Her mother, Kincaid felt, had discarded her when the younger siblings came along. Kincaid soon began building a life of her own, an act of radical autonomy: she found a job in a photo store, started writing, started writing for the *New Yorker*, converted to Judaism, started writing novels, leading her to us, to her readers. In an interview, she once said that when she was ten, her French teacher shoved *Jane Eyre* in her hands to read as a punishment for disrupting the class. She says: '*Jane Eyre* transformed my life...I started to think the possibility of living outside the prescribed life. And my prescribed life was I was a servant.'

Jane Eyre is a book that transforms the lives of many girls unhappy with their station. Badly behaved and hungry girls. Well-behaved girls find their pleasures and permissions elsewhere. On her arrival in New York, Kincaid was five foot seven inches. Within two years she was just shy of six feet. 'Certain things I had left home with, I outgrew rapidly,' she says. 'One of them was the feeling that I would always be this person, my mother's daughter. I quickly outgrew that. And in this state I became a person who could write, who wanted to write.'

...

In the eighteenth house, I learned to write, or learned to imagine that I would be a writer. To sit at a desk, or stand by it, and not leave until something was achieved. To comprehend money as a tool for securing empty time for this process. Live poor. Reconfigure self-worth differently from friends with jobs and relationships that mattered much more than my own. The lonely labour of it. Unimaginable time. The cost of my room, in this crumbling haven, was three hundred and thirty-three dollars a month, the same as it had been for fifteen years before I arrived. A third of what friends who lived in sharehouses round the corner paid. Without the archaic lease, there would be no writing. At least, none of my own.

In the eighteenth house, I learned to discipline space. Not the communal spaces, which were beyond human control. But my room, my own room, with the black mould blooming across the ceiling. Trapped there for so many dead hours, writing, not writing, I polished and arranged my glass *objets* with neurotic glee, trimmed and wiped the fronds of tropical plants, swept beneath every dark underside. Light stabbed through my window pane onto a prim arrangement: tiny golden echidna. Marbled glass egg. A chain of nasturtiums cascading along the edge of my desk. I washed and sunned my white sheets every Saturday morning.

'I don't know where you came from,' my parents would say when they came to visit. People I brought home, however, were impressed. A boyfriend deduced from it that we could never live together; that if you followed the nasturtiums' tendril to its source, you'd find there a twisted madness. And he was right. My aspiration, so sharp it felt immoral, to own a white monad of my own, pin photos to the walls that no landlord could ever take from me, install cupboards with my bare, unskilled hands—this was the opposite of the animal woman lurking inside me, the one who threatened sometimes to take over.

This Australian is passionate about property.

To have a place to transform and not have to leave. Which is the spiritual end to private property. (A Jesuit friend once said, 'When you leave a place, really *leave*.' A sentiment that fills me with unease.)

...

The adage 'property is theft' is something of a provocation. I heard my parents say it when I was little, and took it then as a given. Coined by the anarchist Pierre-Joseph Proudhon in 1840, it has been applied by Marxists and anarchists to suggest that, at best, private property operates against the principle of human equality. It suggests that, at its worst, property is the means and material of exploitation. Is there a place on earth where this is truer than Australia?

Australians are passionate about property.

In the sixth house, actually a medium-density townhouse, a mushroom sprouted from between the laundry sink's broken tiles. The place had been handed down through a decade of first-house-out-of-homers. My older brother introduced me into the system. My brother, who thought that maybe if you tipped a pot of old lentil soup out in the backyard, lentils might sprout. The more desperate the housemates' financial circumstances, the longer they stayed. Many of the original house keys were missing, and quite a few of the doors could be easily opened using a credit card, front door included. None of the windows had flyscreens. Nothing ever smelled right. Five of us crammed into a three-bedroom townhouse—Cat lived in the garage. But I paid something between fifty-five and seventy-five dollars a week—as much as I could then afford—and the location was *primo*. Eventually, the landlords, who'd never invested in the upkeep of the property—how could they?—found a loophole and kicked us out, slapping us with a three-grand bill.

In the circles I run in, it is considered improper to not bring any landlord horror stories to the party. What are you—a prince?

I imagine the people on the other side of the town, or maybe just a street away, whose dinner-party capital hangs on horror-story *renters*.

What Proudhon says is that private property, here meaning the possession of real estate for the purpose of profiting from rents, produces an asymmetrical power relation between landlord and tenant. Asymmetrical power relations produce despotism. Property, Proudhon writes, is 'the right to use [something] by his neighbour's labour'. Or in other words: to 'live as a proprietor, or to consume without producing, it is necessary, then, to live upon the labour of another'. Of San Francisco's rapid gentrification, Jarett Kobek writes: 'Gentrification was what happened to a city when people with an excess of capital wanted their capital to produce more capital while not attributing any value to labor.'

Those who don't own real estate—renters in Australia are a fine example—find their lives occurring between mouldy walls; they pack up and move biennially; moreover, they pay handsomely for the privilege of paying off another person's debt. These indignities, it could be said, act as a strong incentive for individuals to strive to possess property of their own. Much rarer do we see these indignities act as a catalyst for upending the despotic relations that are born of inequality.

And yet. *Property is theft!* In Australia, it is bloody, violent theft. There is no property without invasion; colonial theft precedes all other thieving. The date of the initial theft is enshrined in the calendar for everyone to see. Unabashed. This first act was an act of despotism, and so every act made thereafter, in its name, could only be violent: invasion, rape, massacre, starvation, infection, miscegenation; incarceration, assimilation, appropriation.

Are these violent tides arbitrary or are they by design? The answer depends on how and where you dwell.

...

The fifteenth house, the *apartment*, was shared with another couple with whom we rarely spoke. The entire Tokyo building swayed like a ship some nights. After a quake I'd lie awake, refreshing the news until the report came in. Only a four-point-two. A three-point-six. A four-point-five. Nothing to worry about. Oh, sure. By the fifteenth house I was fairly sure I'd never stop moving. And I might've been right. In the mornings, the sullen cries of crows. Black coffee. Nude, blanched, winter trees. I ran and ran around that lonely city. Around the grounds of the Imperial Palace, at whose foot lay snapping turtles. Primordial arseholes.

They can bite through a human finger, he told me. I believed him, about almost everything. Unlike most of it, the finger thing was true.

...

Adorno writes, in *Minima Moralia*, that 'The house is past. The bombings of European cities, as well as the labour and concentration camps, merely proceed as executors, with what the immanent development of technology had long decided was to be the fate of houses.' But new houses were built and apartments crept up and over the skyline. The fate of houses was to become *housing*. A rational perversion of what should be a place to live (instead it is a place to exist).

...

The nineteenth house, tall and slender, with pale, glossy tiles on every surface. Two rooms on each floor; bedrooms? Despite the fluorescent strips lighting them, their stark officiary feel, bedrooms are what they became. There I lived as if alone, though I was surrounded by my many housemates. All of us, strangers in Saigon. All of us, longing for the freedom promised, for Christ's sake, of being alone. The bonds I developed in the nineteenth house were single-use and mutually disposable. I went out when I felt like it and returned without notice. When I did have friends visit, I smuggled them into my room, not because the other housemates would object to my having guests, necessarily, but because I objected to the existence of any possible judgement by any possible person. One of my more frequent visitors, who sat somewhere between friend, enemy and lover, incurred a positive review from one housemate. After that I pulled myself further from view.

In the nineteenth house, I wrote a play about sexual obsession, the kind that could only be written in the absence of real sex, *sex* sex. That could only be read in the absence of sex, amid a deracinated appetite. The air out on my tiny balcony, which was wide enough only to stand and smoke a cigarette on, was languid, tropical. Out there I'd watch the men in the upscale wood-panelled restaurant across the laneway: a regal place where members of the Party, red lanterns strung across the open air above them, were served steamed chicken by thin, bare-legged young waitresses. Dust in the afternoon sun, then the clouds swelling into an eruption. Though that latitude colours my face mauve, chafes raw my inner thighs, I miss it all the time. No home there, but freedom from home's talons. When eventually I felt the bonds tangle and tighten, I left.

...

In the twenty-second house, I live alone. I live with you. The walls are white, aerial. No one calls. I eat when I am hungry. Go to sleep and wake early. This morning, though, I thought I heard someone knock on our front door. An anxiety rose in me, though I can't explain why. You opened it, but no one was there. I was relieved. Though this longing for isolation, this enjoyment of it, induces a guilt feeling.

...

A few months ago, I read a feel-good—or maybe it was horrifying—news story about an elderly couple in Rome who found themselves so despairing with loneliness they wept and wept until the neighbours called the state police. Four officers knocked on the door and made the couple spaghetti with parmesan to soothe them. One officer described the encounter: 'Sometimes the loneliness melts into tears. Sometimes it's like a summer storm. It comes suddenly and overtakes one.'

I thought, I don't want to live through that. But also, I thought, how many millions of people are sitting in their apartments right now with no reprieve from their isolation? I've had peace and privacy, living without a hundred housemates with a hundred opinions, for three months out of my three decades. I cherish this quiet, this long-awaited solitude. But for many, aloneness, for years, and involuntary, unkind—that's a different story. Millions of people not kept busy enough to assuage this dread.

...

My parents raised me to believe in incredible busyness. Really adhere to it. An idle afternoon is still, for me, a cause for self-flagellation. Not so unusual in this busy world. 'Busywork' might be the word. Busy/work. Because there are so many conveniences to a life where I am from. Growing up we didn't offer our busy-ness to weave cloth for the winter, we did not churn butter nor make candles nor pluck animal corpses nor walk miles to send a message. We were catching the train to school we were walking the dogs we were memorising our lines we were queueing up at the supermarket we were stirring in the mincemeat we were waiting to be picked up from soccer we were rinsing the plastic-bagged spinach we were mopping. We were tramming to part-time jobs we were meeting friends for coffee we were searching for missing library books we were calling Mardi we were watching *Law & Order*. This whole time, any one of us could have sat in our rooms and read the dictionary, or the Bible, or learned a language from scratch and no one would have noticed. Could have lived off dried beans and potatoes, some leaves from the garden, a chicken once a month. But we lived instead as we were supposed to, which is to say we lived according to the prin-ciple of industriousness.

Once it is installed, the belief in the need to always be pain-fully useful, but not really *helpful*, it is unshakeable. (Annie Dillard: 'How we spend our days is, of course, how we spend our lives.') We live where we live so that we can go to work and be useful. We endure gendered labour divisions so that we can help others to be useful. We endure endless boredom and repetition at our jobs indebted to this belief. When we are 'out of work' we lose motivation, feel worthless, start sleeping nine, ten hours a night. When we feel worthless we leave our sheets on the bed until they are dank. We eat too many simple carbohydrates, we drink, we lose faith in our unrealised abilities.

We consume according to how much our particular busyness is valued against other people's *business*. We consume according to how valued our business is against other businesses. Or we consume according to the status of our dead ancestors, whose money is the spoils of other people's dead ancestors' labour, labour which was, often, never paid for.

Religion is not too close to me, not really, not in terms of worship, yet here I am, a lapsed bad Catholic, caught in the larger culture of what Max Weber named the Protestant work ethic. Weber describes Calvin's doctrine of predestination: that only a select few mortals are chosen to join God in heaven after death. And its connection to industriousness: knowing of predestination, the only way a person can live with hope is to *believe* that they have been chosen, and so live life faithfully to honour this birthright—work like a dog to prove your pre-selection was a sensible choice of God's. 'In its extreme inhumanity,' writes Weber, 'this doctrine must above all have had one consequence for the life of a generation which surrendered to its magnificent consistency …A feeling of unprecedented inner loneliness.'

This work ethic, which is my work ethic, makes it a moral duty to pursue the drudgery of daily labour. In the Calvinist framework, becoming 'successful' in a particular professional field—or simply successfully accruing wealth—is a sure sign of having been chosen after all. If success does not arrive from a person's 'good works', this is a clear indication they are not among the chosen; to not even try would be sacrilege.

...

The best place to live is nowhere. *Nowhere*. Nowhere is the only place that is unconstrained by ideology, untainted by any terrible history. Nowhere is the only place where you can step on the ground and not disturb old graves, old horrors. *Nowhere* does not project the picture of your future. It's only in Nowhere that you can be in the moment; in Nowhere, time has no objects nor movement to mark itself against. Nowhere, you are in the midst of immortal blessings. That's Epicurus: 'For man loses all semblance of mortality by living in the midst of immortal blessings.'

Perhaps Nowhere is a fugue state, a state of primeval being, the flow state you enter when you focus for so long your body doesn't exist and you're just pure kneading or pedalling or fucking.

The worst place to live is Australia. Or maybe that's taking it too far.

...

The eighth house, I am saying *house* again but this too was an apartment, was in what was supposedly the last remaining building of the Warsaw ghetto. Two months? I don't know, four? I didn't pay the rent. The place was owned by a friend, well, his parents owned the place, and this friend and his girlfriend and their several pet rats stayed always in their bedroom. When his girlfriend went home to Bristol, my housemate forgot to eat for several days and the rats began to smell putrid. I spent my days in Warsaw more or less alone, walked around the old 'Palace of Culture and Science', aka Stalin's birthday cake, *ha-ha*, and came home to wrap myself in blankets inside the old, grand apartment. When my boyfriend came home, we'd talk, wrapped up on the lounge bed we slept in, or we'd go see an old movie at the film club for just two złoty. Some mornings a tour group of American Jews would come into the building's courtyard, with only cameras separating them from the concrete walls that had imprisoned their people. At night, I dreamed I was raped by Nazis.

These Warsaw days were long and empty: I couldn't find work teaching English, so I read and got bored of reading; I cooked; I sat at the kitchen table and sketched the fruit bowl, badly, waiting for the boy I was there for to come home. I was out of money, so I spent nothing. I thought, then, I would become an artist.

How could I know there would be no epiphany?

On a tram one day, a friend pointed out the Powązki Cemetery and the Jewish cemetery that abuts it. The graves of the Jewish dead were all cloaked in long grass or consumed by vines. The headstones that were visible were moss-soaked and crumbling, tumbling over. Seeing this decrepitude, I was overcome with sadness. There is no one left to look after them, my friend said. A small Jewish population still lives in the city, of course, but it's surely not their responsibility—a few thousand individuals—to safeguard the legacy of the millions of dead, dead and murdered. Surely, I thought, the legacy of Jewish people in Poland concerns the Polish legacy, too; though the 'ethnic' Poles may have, mostly, forsaken their Jewish brothers. In 2018, Poland passed a law making it illegal to 'accuse' the Polish nation or state of complicity in the Holocaust. Yet there are four hundred years, or five—some say a millennium—of Jewish life within the nation.

Psalms 91 begins:

1. Whoever dwells in the shelter of the Most High will rest in the shadow of the Almighty.

2. I will say of the Lord, 'He is my refuge and my fortress, my God, in whom I trust.'

This messianic psalm is about positioning the spiritual life above the life of the flesh. It goes on: 'If you say, "The Lord is my refuge"…no harm will overtake you.' The psalms are liturgical prayers, meaning that they are for public worship. The origins of the synagogue occurred in exile, so say some scholars; synagogues, after the destruction of Jerusalem, could come into being with just ten men in a space they claimed for worship. It is impossible to ignore the connection of these two things: a people made a perpetual kind of refugee by racism, forced from home after home; and the trembling knowledge that this material world could never deliver a stable sense of real belonging. In the case of Jewish exile, this connection is true, it is material. But its truth says something to me too.

I have my doubts, though, about whether, with the inheritance I have, which is rational which is Western which is 'sceptical', I am allowed even imaginary access to this spirit world. Unlike exiles of the recent past, who, without a home had at least a tradition, faith, a stable spiritual home to dwell in, I am instead destined to find home only in mortar and rootlessness.

But then again, what is an interior life if not a chorus of invisible ghosts shouting at one another: parents and siblings and friends and lovers and teachers and enemies and masters and every novel newspaper celebrity and the dead, all of the dead. What is history if not a stunted, haunted conversation between the living and the dead? Inviting the dead into the world of the living is finding a way to be at home in the body, which is not only a body made of skin and bones. A body that exists only because it exists in relation to the deceased bodies that have created it.

I don't have to romanticise an ontology I have no access to (say, early Jewish spiritualism) in order to witness the non-material world. Indeed, the 'ancestors' and the 'communities' we believe we have shucked off (where I come from, at least) are still present. They haunt us, not least because they make it possible for us to be alive. And maybe knowing this might make it imaginable for me, now, to find a kind of home that is rich and interior and not connected to buildings or wealth or authorised belonging. One that is perhaps, for the first time, respectful of the living and the dead.

Notes to Unlived Time

> *Unlived time, the part of time*
> *that can never belong to us...*
> —Bhanu Kapil

Four months into my stay in Germany I realise I have been wearing the same heavy coat every day for more than twelve months. A faded, used-to-be-black London Fog I bought at a thrift store for twenty-five dollars. Every day for more than a year, because I moved to a new hemisphere. How long can a person purely winter, I think; how many blue-black days can she endure without cracking it.

The chill stirs up my longing for warm bare-leggedness. Fake-tanned bare-leggedness. Hot itchy days, hot romance nights.

An involuntary memory comes as I walk across Winter-feldtplatz, carefully, avoiding iced puddles. A night I stayed in summer Sydney with J, who I was losing my mind over. I was twenty-three and he tall, slender, older enough for me to go soft for. I identified him by the character he liked to play: the Intellectual, which I liked playing at, too. Wanted to impress him so much, and the way to do that was by keeping my mouth shut. At the cinema we saw *Melancholia* by Lars von Trier and walked back to my place in the dark wet heat. Street lights illuminated the front-yard plants all glossy and thick-stemmed alien. Cockroaches crawled out from every crevice, scuttled across the pavement. A feeling, biblical. 'Are you supposed to kill them?' I asked him as I crushed one under my blue suede sandal. 'So juicy,' I said. 'Seems wrong.'

We talked in a civilised tone about the film, me pretending I was an A-plus student by birth, *lah lah lah*, me pretending I was knowledgeable about the cinematic arts enough to be loved by him, when my only real observation was that I'd never seen depression rendered so true. We avoided the obvious, though, because I suppose he was tricking me into loving him too. This was during that period of mania for the other that sometimes happens and which disturbs sleep.

What would I be if I had stayed with that man.

Every time I looked at his neck I thought *guillotine*, it was that thin.

...

All elements align for work to ensue. Except for the main ingredient: will. Instead, I read emails from four-to-ten years ago. I keep my old emails, keep the passwords to old accounts. I tell myself this is for work, the work of writing memoir, which might be the same as sentimentality, or laziness. I revisit old emails more frequently than I am emotionally equipped for. I read one from the man whose neck I thought about slicing; over two years, he and I created a vast archive of correspondence; each email longing for the next. When I rifle through these old ruins, my heart starts jumping. Not because of the long-forgotten names, the lovers I can't for the life remember loving, the former cohabitants who no longer circuit my existence. Although there is that. I shudder because of the plans I made—and documented—and then never fulfilled. The voice from the past that was so desperate for a future. Whose voice is that?

I read an email where I declare to the recipient that I am writing a novel (no idea what about). I am making an anthology of contemporary manifestoes. I am considering moving to Montreal. I am starting a radical university for writers and thinkers that has nothing to do with *the* University.

It's touching, I suppose, to see myself like that, a girl of future action. But mostly there is chagrin circling the absence of my follow-through. Fantasy futures not lived, having never lived.

...

On Sunday Dom and I slugged around in bed all day. Early love days, cocooned in faith for the future. I made a salad we heated up the leftover lasagne we watched maybe three films in a row and fucked in the style of cinematic love making. Except I was bleeding so there were more paper towels.

The first time there had been blood, too. We'd spent the day glued together, not yet kissing, then walked at midnight touching hands. We sat on the steps in front of a church, the new brick kind that lets sun in through huge yellow windows, and talked about the books we loved and hated, inflecting our readings with more seriousness than *you move me*, and we talked about the kinds of relationships we'd been in before and how they hadn't worked because of the highly specific ways we envisioned spending our days. Not the slug days, but the work days, and the warm sensation struck I could five-years-into-the-future the sensation of holding his hand and curling his hair his ear love.

A tousled ginger cat marched quickly before us across the street, little ginger paws motoring madly beneath its body. And a few beats later three foxes marched after it—two luxuriant fur tails, one missing a chunk—jogging with the same urgency as the cat but not breaking into a sprint, which led me to believe the fox crew was not there to murder the cat but to collude with him or her on a midnight mammal project.

This may well have been my first urban fox sighting, but I can never really differentiate between what I've seen with my body, in time and space, and what I've seen on TV and later revisited in a dream. It's becoming a problem: have I ever really seen a killer whale?

The point is that this staunchly European sighting elated me so I turned and kissed this man I thought I would love for at least five years and it was rather uncoordinated but still we went back home and my blood was thickly hot and crimson and within minutes the scene was butchery yet overall primitively hot.

...

When I teach writing, I sometimes encounter a question I don't always know how to answer. It goes like this: *but why should we write? Why write, when there is so much horror going on in the world?*

Privately, I think: what has horror got to do with writing or not writing? I think: there is sweetness in the world, too, and scatological humour. There is time in the day. Enough time, maybe, for everything. I think, my inner curmudgeon revealing herself: if there is time for binge drinking and spin class and pets, there is time enough for writing.

I say, more often than not: let's take this excellent question to the class, shall we?

This doubting student might only be spoiling for a fight, uninterested in books or writing and looking to justify her prejudices. But she might also be a doubting writer, an earnest one, seeking only a witness, an accomplice, a nod of the head at just the right time, someone to confirm: it's allowed, you're allowed to write and you're allowed to read despite—or because of—the horror.

The first time I fielded this question I was unprepared. There was no evidence I could call on to prove the virtue or vice of reading or writing. Literature is not a 'pure' thing, not by any stretch; it does not arrive from a white monad. It's conditioned by the materials of its production, the ideological constraints of time, place, power, personality. It is historically contingent, sometimes awfully so. Alan Liu writes that 'the churning of literary capital has always characterized literature. Literature could not have been part of the life of culture otherwise.' Is this what the (now hypothetical, purely rhetorical) student is speaking to when she questions the act of writing? The 'churning of literary capital'? Does the doubter mean: why write, when literature has so often helped naturalise—rather than expose or challenge—harmful ideologies?

That is: the horror right now. A mass extinction event; ten million stateless people on earth; crop death; the resurgence and mainstreaming of fascism. Add to this road rage. Add to this weak teabags. Add to this cheating spouses; period pain; rude customers; missing library books; bank fees; the privatisation of health care; the existence of real-estate agents. I don't want to be the one to stand at the head of a classroom and argue that what the world needs right now is another book-object, made with seriousness and care, printed on dead trees and transported with fossil fuels, circulated endlessly between naughty, horror-avoidant humans like me. But every action contains an argument. My standing in the classroom is itself an argument, and I am responsible for the arguments I make.

Why write? Especially about something as trivial as the particularities of one's own creature thoughts, habits or obsessions? My timeline fills with these endless 'debates' about what the hell a person is now, about how 'self-representation' fares in the internet age. Is the personal essay a corrupt form? (Possibly.) Does social media promote narcissistic behaviour? (I suppose.) Is 'self-care' a neoliberal scam promoting individualistic coping strategies in the absence of broader social obligations or the possibility of radical structural change? (Well, yes, I say to myself as I slip into my fourth late-night bath of the week, thinking about my next semester of unemployment.)

So I make notes in preparation for more questions. Now when the student raises her hand and asks, in a voice tinged with cruelty or boredom or curiosity or desire, 'But *why?*', I will say:

+ Because there is a human future; maybe not a forever-future, but one beyond now. Writing is an argument for hope: it believes in the future; it believes, even, in futures it ought to know better than to. It believes in the ongoingness, the wanton tenacity, of human beings.

+ Because the only world we know, we know through the inches of shadowed pink between our ears. Everything is mediated through our spongy, lumpy brains. Writing can't help but demonstrate how dubiously, how erroneously and how enchantingly knowledge is produced, remembered, transmitted.

+ Because one's own shadowy pink matter enfolded in bone is unlike anybody else's. Because this singularity is repeated endlessly: this is the unfolding diversity of the world.

+ Because, as Édouard Glissant writes, 'we change through our exchange with others'. Because writing makes detours from individual truths and desires and dreams. It anticipates and facilitates exchanges between people who were never supposed to meet.

+ Because when I pick up a second-hand book, I hope for a letter inside, or a tram ticket from 1985, or—god willing—a coffee-ringed photograph of a stranger's child.

+ Because when I open a new book I flip straight to the acknowledgements—doesn't everyone? What matters most to me is: what kind of person writes about made-up others? Or writes about ideas to which 'real life' is supposedly subordinate? Or writes the minutiae of their lives, their hearts, their tongues. To whom do they owe their freedom?

...

My freedom to write is owed to a messy, undisciplined mind. I can manage my physical life, mostly: I bathe, I cook, my house and clothes are clean. The files on my laptop, though, offer a more honest window into my unconscious. My laptop, where I spend my waking life, is not so much a 'filing system' as a temporary storage shed jam-packed with empty bleach containers, rolled-up mouldy carpets, an upside-down shopping trolley. All circled by twelve slow-moving blowflies. There are loose 'drafts' everywhere, some of just a line or two or a quote from something I read some time over the past seven years. They are notes, I suppose: trash note archives.

One draft I stumbled on recently: a list of a daily word count from a project I was working on, declaring that I will write four pages a day! Which I sort of did, which is why, when I try to read that project now, parts of it are incomprehensible. Like most writers I cobble together my living from teaching, editing, and a combination of professional and unprofessional writing gigs, other work. That I fail to create and maintain a naming system means to find what I'm looking for I must rifle through tens, hundreds, of files with names like 'Reason (1)' (a letter outlining my ploy to win an extension of my PhD scholarship); 'about two weeks ago' or 'June 4' (documents containing observations from or about the time of their title); 'I like women who take no prisoners' (a document that contains nothing other than the phrase 'I like women who take no prisoners', which I don't know that I do). These are objective correlatives of a fragmented life—of deep, psychic disharmony. No wonder I feel scattered. Why can't I get it together? Why don't I label these correctly, or suggestively? Do I even care if they are ever read again? What is the future, if the present has me over a barrel?

Perhaps, I have thought, the notes are not strictly for revisiting. Perhaps they're artefacts of good intentions. They are the insisted-upon valour of making the (always-broken) promise that they'll be returned to, retrieved, revised. Notes; hope! Their real addressee is time—things being recorded as they pass by, for the future note-reader to recall. Gestures towards a future that will almost certainly not care.

...

I know of an author who is in the early stages of a successful career. The author posted on social media about being contacted by the National Library, who wanted to acquire her personal papers. Humble-brag aside, she was seeking advice: sell now? Or hold on to the documents for a higher bid, which would surely come at some point later in her career? (Banking on the knowledge (the hope) that her career would continue to flourish. Banking on the impossibility of knowing what will come.)

This thought, to me, was horrifying. Incredible, I thought, that there's a kind of person in the world who is playing the long game, perhaps the longest game imaginable; who has been styling notebooks, early ones, from a time before they were of interest to any library, in such a way that a reader in the future could generate from them meaning, or worse: reproduce them in part, or in full. This degree of future planning, with the intention to control time that is yet unlived, seemed masterful and unreal. (Or sensible, if the future is to be taken for the unforgiving entity it is.) Notes as unfinished business, unattended potential, the writing that is closest to life. Which is terrible. Fragments of potential, they attend to the fantasy that effort is not wasted. Like sowing seeds, but without that loving deliberation. A blind, unconscious hope that a fragment of a thought caught in a note might germinate in a natural way, without tending; that it might wiggle down to find a sip of water, catch a slice of sun through the specks of soil and erupt into the light.

...

On weekends, I am trying to make a habit of going to the Schöneberg Flohmarkt. For the caramel pleasure. The erotics of the discarded. Each Saturday the stink of it, dim old furs and fatty wurst and mildew. Clouds of steam out your lungs through your nose. All the almost-not-chipped china. I went today to find materials for collaging. Trying to make a habit of that too, of making things for no good reason. My delight then at the two-euro book stand, aisles and aisles of open cardboard boxes stacked with books in several languages, many of them old art and cinema periodicals. Decided on a budget of maybe ten euros for whatever might look good cut up on my bedroom floor.

This became the most luxuriant joy. Buying armfuls of printed matter indiscriminately.

In the haul, I picked up an art book called *The American Tradition*, a 1959 copy of an art journal, a 1981 edition of the *New Orleans Review*, a catalogue for an exhibition called German Expressionist Film by the Goethe Institute New York, and a stack of cinema and theatre magazines, my favourite of which is simply an abridged version of *King Lear* illustrated in savage colours. The Goethe Institute catalogue contains maybe twenty risograph pages, each one describing a different German interwar expressionist film.

All useless, according to the common sense of utility, yet all of them inspiring in me curiosity and the simplest delight. Delight in the fact that beautiful things made by people forty years ago sit around, bringing pleasure to a stranger in the now. It reminds me of my duty, everyone's duty, to the future. My friends' kids will need in twenty years to find crap like this at the markets so that they can feel held by the hands of past people's future dreams and not feel totally alone.

Later in bed, after reading the *New Orleans Review*, I pulled over my laptop to Where Are They Now the contributors. A few of them had passed away, others were ungoogleable ghosts. Others still were late-career academics at universities I'd never heard of. Unease stirred in me; perhaps I shouldn't have done that. The sense that I was just like any of these literary-journal people, brimming with a hunger outsized only by obscurity. The sense that This Is Your Life and it's small and trivial and it's going to stay that way.

A scene in *I Love Dick* where the narrator describes seeing a photo exhibition, a photographic/oral history of the Lower East

Side. All these artists, she writes, 'living, drinking, working, in their habitat'. She writes that the 'photos were meticulously captioned with the artists' names and disciplines, but 98% of them were names I didn't know.'

Yet everything seems so important in the moment of its production. How else could anyone ever make anything? Did their work, all those hundreds of anonymous artists (in just one city in one time period alone) leave a trace on other memories, living still, curious or painful or rapturous?

In my market copy of the *New Orleans Review* there is an interview with one John Gardner, who was, apparently, a novelist and critic of some acclaim in this era. I say *apparently*, because before turning my eyes to this page I'd never heard his name. The interview made oblique reference to some kind of scandal, which seemed like general knowledge for the readers of this literary journal in 1981. So I searched the internet until I learned that the scandal was that he'd put out a collection of literary essays in 1978 that pissed off his colleagues. That's all. He was a bit of a conservative, maybe, or a bit up-himself. He'd said critical things about the writing of his peers. The scandal made it into the mainstream media, which led to this writer becoming a sort of pariah. If he were still alive and writing, I'd probably find it in my lesser rodent self to hate him too. But then I read that, in 1982, a year after giving this interview, Gardner died in a motorcycle accident a few miles from his home. And all I could feel for him was sadness. Who cares about opinions, gossip, whatever, when bodies are so vulnerable, in search only of love and breath.

Every body reaches into the future to touch someone there.

...

When I was twenty-three, I threw out all of the notebooks and letters that I had accumulated throughout high-school and university. Course notes, love letters, entire exercise books of intense political and emotional treatises I wrote and shared with my best friends in senior school. Partly, it was an issue of storage. I kept having to move house and didn't have a car or long-term storage options. Partly, I wanted to grow up. Which meant breaking with my old addresses to the future. I, in the now-present, the past's future, was not the person those documents addressed. Not anymore! I was smarter, colder, less sentimental than she had been. I was a grown woman, and I was a writer. I dumped everything in several bins on my street on garbage day, and once they were gone, I regretted it painfully.

There was one notebook from that hoard that I kept for a while longer. It contained notes from a short phase during which I thought I had discovered the shortcut to creation: drinking glasses of wine I had not yet acquired a taste for, alone, on my back porch, frantically scribbling what I thought would be poems. I had heard the erroneous claim that lyric poets, like mathematicians, peaked at the age of twenty-one. I was nineteen and worried I'd miss out before I had a chance. Needless to say, the poems were bad. Needless to say, I never touch alcohol now when I write. Eventually, I chucked that notebook, too. By discarding these relics, I was able to turn away from the tussle between my current, past and imagined futures that together so embarrassed me.

If anything of me lives on after I am dead, I hope it will not be what I failed to get done. When I die, when it happens, please throw my MacBook into the ocean.

. . .

Once a week I have a 'comprehensive shower'. To set the record, my body, straight. Slather a mask on my face and, while it cracks, dry body brush my limbs. This is said to aid circulation, though I suspect diet and exercise and whether or not you're breathing have more to do with that. Then shave legs, too-hot shower, exfoliate bodily form, shampoo hair twice. Taps off. Squeeze hair out and run palms across every plane of the body to remove the excess water. A touch of oil on the bleached parts of the hair and wrap it all in a little towel. Dry off limbs, torso, Q-tip ears. Moisturise all over. Some kind of acid on cheeks, forehead, followed by a fine layer of oil. Blow-dry hair and shape it with a flat iron. Spray. BB cream. Eyebrows on. Feel like I look good but no one can tell the difference. Feel guilty, too, for frivolity. Coming as I do from the no-nonsense, Aldi-shopping, carbohydrate-operated economic class, this devotion to grooming seems immoral. Like a vice. If you want luxury, I hear my superego crow, tie oatmeal in a sock and dunk it in the bathtub! Smash a raw egg in your hair. Rinse your locks in vinegar.

Yet secretly I have started buying aspirational oils and serums. A sixty-dollar bottle of what is essentially sunflower oil and lavender. A tiny sticky-pink perfume with a sex-and-drugs name. Victim of the beauty craze lured by a marketing executive's promise of glow eternal, divine. I keep the enchanted little things—blue glass bottle, silver on buttercup-yellow—in dark-corner places, so that visitors don't see the labels, estimate how much they cost and feel invited to make assumptions about the decay of my soul. Other times I find myself wanting to out them; on a good day a visitor might use my bathroom and think, 'decayed or not, this soul cares about the state of her exterior'.

I've heard it argued that the skincare trend is a detour of planetary insecurity: that in a time of impending non-future, consumers enjoy the promise of exercising control over the ravages of time (wrinkles). That, I think, is wishful bullshit. We skincare dupes are mostly women; we live, almost all, in developed, capitalist countries. We may be 'broke', but no one buying overpriced chemical serums is poor. In the absence of other obligations, or in spite of them, we spend what little money we earn on luxuriant bottles of hope against time. Because this is women's consumption, it is invariably enacted in the context of patriarchy. Why smooth skin (aside from its smoothness)? Why, even, youth (aside from its youth)? Any answer to this is conjecture, but that's okay. Women are, I suspect, valued for their proximity to fertility. Fertility is the stand-in for eternally reproducing futures. When women deviate from the appearance of youth, fuckability or fecundity (because of menopause, illness, or transition towards or away from femininity), they violate the social mandate of heteropatriarchal society: to endlessly reproduce the species; to placate anxieties about environmental collapse. Dull and creased skin, women who grow old without intervention, women who refuse beauty, may well function as shocking reminders that futures, like bodies, are not manageable entities.

...

Skin is not just a marketing opportunity or a symbol of regeneration or the source of glow-eternal-divine. It's the container of the past, too. Of all the genetic detours that lead to you.

From my notebook, taken during a lecture given by Marianne Hirsch:

the skin imprinted with actual memories
skin as a media of production
'epidermal memory'
traumatic 'after effects'
sculptural dislocations
childhood and the future - in the same memory
(past futures)
skin as a site of aloneness and connection
'intercorporeality'
mother as an enveloping skin
'skin ego'
skin contains psychic contents
skin and touch as locations of trauma
locked within skin are patterns of care

I typed out these notes and sent them to a friend who had lost half her house—and then her skin-touch sensation—in a terrible cyclone. And then I left my notebook on a plane. With everything I needed to remember. *Gone*.

That notebook, I kept thinking after I lost it, holds the *key*. To my knowing. A couple of good months I don't want to lose memory of. Notes from my reading, self-imposed deadlines never honoured, lists of hypothetical money never earned. Artefacts of good intentions.

Notes, whose real addressee is time, are for a future to regard the past triumphantly. They insist that the future will care. A future self, looking back to a past me looking forward. My notebook, gone.

Nothing, of course, like losing part of your house. What am I saying.

Nothing like losing the sensation of skin-touch.

How do you live a catastrophe without turning to cliché?

(Shut your mouth and look sideways.)

(Or open your mouth and say the wrong thing.)

There are no catastrophes now, not in the middle of these German days I spend alone or with Dom, confined to the apartment while it blizzards out, working, or out walking with Tim, talking about every small thing we have thought of before, talking through the clichés the tongue is tied to.

...

What Elizabeth Hardwick wrote about memories: 'If only one knew what to remember or what to pretend to remember. Make a decision and what you want from the lost things will present itself. You can take it down like a can from a shelf. Perhaps.'

Portrait of the
Writer as Worker
(after Dieter Lesage)

You are a writer and you know what that means: you don't do it for the money. You don't do it for the money, which is a great reason people have to not pay you for your writing. So it happens that you, a writer, invest your money in projects others will feature in their magazines, exhibitions, festivals, reading lists on the internet. You are an investor. You are building a diverse portfolio.

You are living a double life, a friend says to you, a friend who is trying to live a double life of her own and has called you for tips on double-life living. You are living a double life, one where at two p.m. you are in the office of a colleague who is getting paid upwards of two hundred thousand dollars a year and by half-past five you are polishing cutlery before the dinner rush. The dress you are wearing is shapeless and black, a look intended for wealthy women twice your age, a look intended for women who did not just pump the shit up out of a clogged toilet in the student lodgings they are temporarily living in. You are a writer and you know what that means: you are investing your money in your work, which in turn provides employment for other people. You say you are living a double life when you should say you are investing in a diverse portfolio. You are an investor.

Before you assume the title of investor you are a student, providing temporary employment for writer-teachers by enrolling in their creative writing units. You demonstrate almost no talent, which is not the same as no *potential*, or no *future*, but is often thought of in the same breath. Yet there you are, in a class of your peers, some with even less talent than you, and many with much more of it. You go to all the book events you can find out about. You go to these events hoping to catch a glimpse of the writers whose work you read before you knew they also had bodies, writers covered with a fine sheen. You blush when you meet them. You would like to be a literary citizen. You write them emails, some-times, and sometimes they respond. You read *The Red and the Black*. You are disturbed by Julien Sorel's megalomania but can see where he's coming from. Within a handful of years, you will become the writer-teacher, because you are cheaper per hour than your older writer-teachers are; you will—tacitly, grate-fully, occasionally—accept employment indirectly provided by the writer-students enrolled in your class, who yearn to be writer-investors themselves, or else to simply get okay grades in units widely deemed 'a bludge'.

You write some book reviews and columns for the student newspaper. You write an average op-ed for a magazine and get interviewed about it on the radio. Your parents seem impressed. You write more book reviews for magazines your friends are making, which surely no one reads, then you take it upon yourself to lead a workshop for other writers who have not yet written book reviews that will not be read, a workshop on writing book reviews. You are editing the student newspaper. You are an elected student politician. You attend student council meetings and roll your eyes when the various factions clash in highly emotive and largely perverse ways. You organise a conference for student writers. You write short speeches introducing the panellists and speakers emphasising their significance and the importance of collaboration. The speakers do not remember you the next time they see you.

You make dinner to introduce people to one another. You open bottles of wine. You serve variations on the theme of vegetable curry. You talk about what needs to happen. You finish bottles of wine. You are invited to dinner and you are introduced. You are younger than everyone you dine with. And then you are the same age as them. One day you will be older. You pretend you are for real.

You say you are a freelancer. You apply for a receptionist job that pays better than your retail job, which has recently cut your shifts. The receptionist job comes through but the starting date is the same date you're supposed to talk at a writers' conference interstate and you've already paid for the train trip and the hostel, so you go to the conference instead of taking the receptionist job and at the closing party you get high and hand out your business card to everyone you talk to. Your card says that you are a writer. You have no idea why you have such a business card. That night you kiss the friend of the person you actually want to kiss. The person you kiss tells you he is a Deleuzian. He is a philosopher-DJ-conference organiser.

You write some copy for a museum for more money than you've ever earned before and the boss invites you to apply for the job full-time. You ignore her email and with the money you buy a ticket overseas so you can stop diversifying your portfolio for just one second and also be away from people who identify as Deleuzians. You are an international artist. You are writing a play. You have no one overseas to hang out with. You are about to run out of money. You get a job at an English-language nightlife magazine, where you write wrap-ups of exhibition launches and brand launches and musical shows. Your editor, who employed you, she says, because she was drawn to your writing voice, is now highly critical of your writing voice. She says *maybe you don't find all this as cool as you should*. You write her PR fluff in a downbeat ironic voice. You don't know what her problem is. The people you are writing fluff pieces about are artists-photographers-DJs. Some of them, they tell you, are models. They have diverse portfolios. You are not a model. Sometimes you ride round with them on motorbikes and drink fifty-cent beers on their concrete roofs. They invite you to their launch. They tell you they are DJing at their launch. You tell them you'll write about their launch.

You return home with a finished play, which nobody asked you to write, which nobody will ever read let alone produce. You return home with less than a hundred dollars in your bank. Not enough money to go to a friend's wedding. No dress, no present. You stay home and, like that, that friendship is over. You borrow five hundred dollars. You apply for a PhD. You hear the money is amazing. You ask an academic you admire to supervise you. She says yes, even though she knows it is pecuniary factors that have led you to her office.

You are living a double life, you remind your ex-boyfriend after buying three identical black smock dresses that can be worn from a sleepover to a teaching gig to an artist talk to the bar. You forget to eat dinner, so you buy three potato cakes on the way home for two dollars fifty. You are dressed like a middle-aged curator, your ex-boyfriend tells you. You are dressed like a middle-aged curator riding a speedy road bike round the city with your backpack filled with everything you will need for a meeting with a DJ-editor-journalist about an essay you plan to co-author but never do, a trip to the library to check some references, a talk by an arts worker-poet, and then for pho afterwards with a curator-archivist who is not a DJ. You carry a stick of deodorant in your bag. You carry a small bottle of perfume. You have a hundred and twenty-two dollars in the bank.

...

You somehow get into the PhD. The money is amazing. Until it is just normal. Until it is certainly not enough. A man you have been working for on and off for years offers to pay you to write part-time for his online magazine. The magazine is not entirely what you had in mind when you decided to become a writer, but he says he has the money. You go to work two days a week in an office that is part of a design studio. You publish essays on every topic you can muster, four or five a month, essays which have not been copyedited nor proofread, and every fortnight you fight the man to get your pay. The money eventually comes, in dribs and drabs, all of it. Every fortnight you commission and edit two or three stories written by other writers. You are a paid editor. You have a budget to pay other writers money for their writing. This work takes up more than the two days you are paid to work. But now you have your scholarship, too. You have diversified your portfolio. You are an investor.

You write text for an artist friend's video work. You're a collaborator. You write lectures and booklets to hand out at workshops. You're a teacher. You give a lecture in someone's garage about male writing versus female writing. You're a feminist. You pitch book reviews to publications you quietly believe are morally comprised. You're a literary citizen. You present yourself a certain way, and all of a sudden that's what you are. You attend the launch of an art magazine, where you ask an artist to look over your new essay. In return, she asks you to help make work for her upcoming installation. You're a member of an artistic community. You write grants you don't get, and some you do. You write references for younger writers applying for courses and jobs and grants of their own. You buy young poets' chapbooks. Sometimes you even read them. You host literary journal parties. Everyone you know goes to the parties and other parties too. You have a strong feeling that no one at the parties reads the insides of the journal you edit. At these parties you invite people to contribute to the journal whose party you are hosting. Nobody has asked you to do this. Nobody is paying you for it. Your colleague is DJing at the party. Your future ex is at the party with his future ex. Your DJing colleague is diversifying her portfolio. Your future ex is diversifying his.

People you went to university with have their own little magazines now. You give them your writing and agree to read at their launches. You invite them to contribute to your magazine. They read at your launches. You give money to their crowdfunded edition and they give money to yours. You have six dollars left in the bank. You are tired from the deadlines for the jobs done overnight to fit it all in. Your right shoulder is sore. Your median nerve is fried. Your boyfriend doesn't give you massages. You break up with your boyfriend. The man who is now your ex-boyfriend starts giving you massages.

You are a writer and you know what that means. You're not doing it for the money. You are not doing it for the money, which is a great reason people have to not pay you.

You wear shiny shorts and a Margiela top to a fundraiser for an activist collective. Your bra is visible. Everyone's bra is visible. It's that kind of an activist collective. All of the activists are DJs.

Some of them, they say, are also writers. You introduce yourself and invite the activist-DJs to submit to your magazine. On the way home, you listen to a lecture series about early Christianity. You go home to finish reading Andrea Dworkin's first book, which is different from what you expected. You are diversifying your practice.

You apply for international residencies. In your applications you recycle the garbled grantspeak phrases you are starting to know better than you know your own work. You attach a folio of your work, which has no real aesthetic unity because you have been diversifying your portfolio for years now. Your portfolio is read by RZA, who is on the board of an international residency you applied for. You do not get into the international residency that RZA is on the board of.

You are late for the launch party of the magazine you edit. You are exhausted and slightly ill and it is midwinter, yet it is crucial that you are there. You spend thirty-five dollars on a cab fare and you get one free drink at the bar. You introduce yourself to someone who says you've been introduced before and so quickly you introduce them to someone else. You are a writer and you know what that means: you are a maître d'. You work hard, but do you work smart? No one is paying you for this. Your colleague is DJing the party. Someone you haven't been introduced to is taking photos at the party. You introduce yourself. You and she are in this together. Perhaps you are even collaborators.

...

You collaborate with an artist on a performance work. You perform it together at a prestigious art space. A dancer approaches you, says *we should collaborate*. You never hear from the dancer again. An artist uses your work to accompany her video work. She does not attribute the text or audio recording to you. She does, however, take your author portrait for you and never invoices for it. There's an artist you long to collaborate with but you can't imagine dragging her into this. She is another kind of investor. You go to the launch of a young poet's chapbook. You don't recognise any of the faces, the faces all covered with a fine layer of subcutaneous fat and optimism. One of the poets starts DJing.

You work hard but do you work smart? You resign from publications. Nobody notices. You are a researcher now. Maybe you are a poet too. You are an editor, paid to proofread masters theses in all areas of the humanities. You are a collaborator. You are not a DJ. You are presenting your work within a research context. You go to an academic conference and swap emails with early-career researchers.

Your parents no longer know what you do for a living. Do you have a job? they ask. They know you are busy. You are on Twitter. Too busy to come over for lunch on Sunday. People you met at uni now have real jobs. They are no longer writer-investors. They tell you how expensive life gets after you get a real job, how the price of a nice mattress is really quite steep. You wouldn't know. You quit Twitter. Some of your peers now work in comms or advertising or arts administration. Maybe they are working on some unified future writing. Not you. You are a writer, and you know what that means: you don't do it for the money. You don't do it for the money, which is a great reason people have to not pay you for your writing.

Antimemoir, as in, Fuck You (as in, Fuck Me)

> *Often I think that writing is a*
> *futile effort; so is reading; so is living.*
> —Yiyun Li, *Dear Friend,*
> *from My Life I Write to You in Your Life*

> What was the chief part of an orator? *He answered,*
> action: *what next?* action: *what next again?* action.
> —Francis Bacon, 'Of Boldness'

Stones underfoot: they're slope-faced, many thousands of them, ancient as the moon. They crunch as she hobbles over them from the water's edge towards the castle. She should have worn her runners. Up ahead, Kronborg Castle—Elsinore, for today—is as vast and regal as any castle. The scene is so familiar, though how could it be? It's her first time in Denmark.

    —You didn't go to Kronborg that day.

    —Let me do this. My way.

    —This is fiction!

    —A frame.

The performance of *Hamlet* begins under the great white banner of the sky; scene by scene, the actors work their way through the halls and chambers and grounds of the castle. At each scene change, she follows the audience-herd around to the next set—which is just the castle, the castle is the set is the castle.

Every year, a new season of *Hamlet* is staged at Kronborg.

Must be a great gig for the actors, she thinks.

> —Rather, she imagines she'd have thought, had she been there…

'One season,' a Dane told her, 'Jude Law played the role of Hamlet. It was like the biggest thing to happen in Denmark.'

No Jude Law this time. Just actors with dark eye make-up smeared, whose faces seem, as all the Danes do, vaguely familiar to her. White people of a certain variety, the planes of their faces suggestive of her own and her brothers': broad foreheads, small, round noses. Invasions a millennia old alive in the angles of their jaws, the licks of pale hair at their temples. 'Viking', she later learns on Wikipedia, doesn't describe an ethnic group. Not the red-headed. Not the burly fleshed. Viking is just another word for marauder. Genetic memories, arbitrarily, violently implanted.

Though 'Viking Queen' does have a ring more charming than 'Pillaging Monarch'.

> What a piece of work is a man! How noble in reason, how infinite in faculty, in form and moving how express and admirable, in action how like an angel, in apprehension how like a god—the beauty

of the world, the paragon of animals! (*Hamlet*,
act 2, scene 2)

—*And yet to me, what is this quintessence of dust?*

—Oh, Hamlet. Hamlet and the pillaging monarchs.
The forms upon which 'the human', *humanity*,
that concept, that ideology, is based. Just a pile of
worthless dust.

She exits the castle early. Gets on a train back to the flat grey
city. Enough Shakespeare for one day. Though she is in Copen-
hagen for a summer school on world literature—and *Hamlet*
is *the* work of world literature, the work with multiple sources
and endless articulations, adaptations—she hates the play: the
wronged prince, the dead crazy girl, and in this instance—

—*This imaginary instance—*

the pompous black-cloaked production values.

And these days, all castles look like Trump Tower to her.

—*Truth time.*

—Okay.

—*You didn't go.*

—I didn't. But, let me—

—She didn't really go to Kronborg Castle that day.

She was supposed to go on the *Hamlet* excursion, a voluntary
activity organised by the summer school she was attending. She
should have (could have) been a good sport and gone along. But
castles aren't all that, and neither is *Hamlet*. And besides, the

summer school had caused her to reel in mild horror—for days at a time—at the institution, the roles and rules, of academia. So instead of attending the play, she, and he, took the train across the bridge to Malmö, sweet little Swedish city, to visit a friend.

—A true story.

—*Why not?*

In Malmö that day, while the poor summer-school students went out to see a sad play, the friends went to a green park and watched a band perform. The singer, a new Swede from old Iraq, told a true love story from the shores of Greece, where she had first arrived in Europe.

—*How true?*

—Stories of love are always true stories.

The tale was simple. Two strangers met at the littoral, on a ribbon of sand between two lives they hadn't yet chosen. Something sparkled right away, something like love, but the two were splintered apart before love could fuse them together. A year later, their bodies met again and completed the act of it, the falling in love of it.

After the concert, they ate smoked eggplant with pomegranate seeds on top, scooped it up with hot round circles of bread. Drank a beer in a garden pub full of revellers who all knew their friend's name and stopped to say hello. Went to sleep at their friend's place, on his bed, with him on a mattress laid out beside them.

—*Better than* Hamlet.

—The best.

   ...

'Memories, images,' Italo Calvino once said, 'once fixed in words, are erased.'

   ...

I met this Malmö friend in Lisbon, where I was writing a rupture from years before. He was there to see a friend of mine, A, his best friend from back home—a great dusty city, which had exiled them both several years before. A holiday. Both friends had been pushed from their homes, torn apart by catastrophe, split apart by lives they had not yet chosen. He to Sweden, A to Germany. They had arranged a room in the Lisbon hills, to fuse together again.

While I was there, at the residency, I met an American artist, B, who was tracing her own ruptured lines, too. In beautiful, yellow Lisbon, city of faded opulence, whose grandeur is due, in part, in large part, to the bones that rest at the bottom of the Atlantic. Where it is impossible to look at the shimmering water without seeing the Middle Passage. (The Middle Passage, the first and greatest trauma on which the era of humanism, of Hamlet's angst, of the ascendance of white skin to the top of the labour chain, is built.) The American artist's lines were drawn from Goa, which had been taken, raided and used by the Portuguese empire for three centuries. When she looked at the glittering ocean, she, too, saw the ships. The American artist listened to me talk about my project, and offered me her copy of the poet Bhanu Kapil's *The Vertical Interrogation of Strangers*. This book is Kapil's first, and is as far as I know out of print. She gave it to me anyway. In it, I found answers to my questions—and the answer wasn't me. The answer wasn't single, nor was it what I longed for. In

Vertical Interrogation, Kapil asks twelve questions. The worst of them: 'Who is responsible for the suffering of your mother?' (A trick question: she's only *my* mother to *me*. But the responsible I is too much to answer to.)

> —Right book at the right time.

> —Is like the right friend inviting you to stay with them a night.

> —Is like the true story of letting love in, despite the distance.

I became obsessed with Kapil. Bought and read her books, read her blog and the anthologies she had contributed to, among them an edition of *Chain* from 2000 titled *Memoir/Antimemoir*. Saw that she had scheduled a free 'Antimemoir and Charcoal' workshop at a gallery in London. Looked up flights—forty-euro tickets there, twenty-seven back. So. A couple of months later in Spitalfields, I met Kapil in her flesh. She wore a cotton dress with a full skirt. Cuban-heeled boots. Leather jacket. Big hair and laughter, too.

For the next three hours, she said once we'd sat down, *I am yours. I am devoted. To you.*

This woman, I thought. And then she led a guided meditation.

She sent us off with reams of white paper and sticks of charcoal to 'free draw' sprawled out on the floor of the gallery. This process, she said, might help us unblock a pattern, a repressed emotion, a shape, for a project that might otherwise be going nowhere.

On the floor of the sunlit gallery, I rocked the base of the charcoal cylinder along the paper's surface, rolled its edge to make a
long coil of crescent moons. Formed a couple of mounds to one
side. And dots surrounding the structure, like pollen in still air,
gently spilling outwards, upwards.

>—*Like spring snow.*

As each student taped their creation to the gallery's walls for
crits, I realised I had drawn a great throbbing cock. When it
was my turn to have the drawing analysed, the other students
said words like:

>—fertile

>—fecund

>—pollinate.

Some bodies don't somatise, Kapil said.

And others are purely somatic, I thought, looking at my cock.

>...

When I returned to the apartment where I lived, I realised I had
a few weeks of spare afternoons coming up, so I decided to use
them to organise some of my work, small essayistic things, into
a hypothetical book proposal.

>—*But. Why?*

>—To somatise?

>—To let the pollen fertilise. To insist on the structure
>of my world.

Hey, said the swinging, smiling, author me of the book proposal. *You can bet on me to write a thought-provoking commercially successful essay collection!*

——Inwardly, of course, my shame.

——*Dickhead.*

I tried to think intentionally about the whole of them, these essays, collected, and the why. Were they essays? Were they memoirs? Was there a difference between the two?

The things were referential, pointed to my real, fleshy time on earth, from the arc of the existence bestowed on me by my ancestors, filtered through the imperfect cadence of language. But was my life a complete one, with a story to tell? Was I a serious enough person to call my work *autotheory*? (No.) Should anyone care about the small line of vision that I am entitled to narrate?

...

'All the images will disappear,' writes Annie Ernaux.

...

In selecting what to write down, what to include, one makes silence of all else. A shadow, or an outline.

——*You consecrate silence.*

Of all the lies told by and about writers, the biggest of them is that the truth is articulable; that it is the writer's hallowed vocation to 'name the world' and in naming it, to remake it.

——Instead, the writer makes the world silent.

I only know spots and silence about my ancestors. Except for the gossip, which is the same as myth. When the last of my grandparents died, not so long ago, I felt history foreclose on me. My link to the living past was gone, and I had done nothing to salvage it while it was still possible.

The grandfathers were not there to begin with—one dead for many years, the other, living, but not for long, on the other side of the world. It was the grandmothers I lost. They had been there; had been somewhat there. But I didn't know them. Not at all. What were these old women like? Who had they been? Who were the girls and young women and middle-aged women that lived inside them? These carriers of all my potential and all my foibles, too.

> —*Damaged people, traumatised, if you believe their children.*

> —I do.

What was their world?

> —*Bad things. Terrible things. Things worse than Trump.*

> —Every unhappy history is unhappy in its own way.

Some of the things that are remembered, mythologised. These women I didn't know.

> She remembers feeling jealous of the Italian women in the maternity ward who, unlike her, were permitted to make noise while they gave birth. They raged. They screamed. She kept it to herself.

She could have been a pianist, she had said, she had said. But the piano, her lifeline, was gambled away by her father when she was still a girl.

A baby at twenty, twenty-one. An unhappy marriage. Too young. Too much life yet to live.

Her beloved cousin's suicide, which no one told her about until after the funeral. So that she wouldn't, couldn't, make a scene.

The six—or was it seven—miscarriages.

Her great rebellion, going to art school, away from home, five years of drawing life, and breasts and cocks and legs and eyes, of falling in love with the young art teacher. Their long walks around the harbour. When she graduated, her mother burnt all her artwork.

Their cotton dresses. Homemade. Before factory clothing.

The era of pants for women to wear to work.

A migration. A cut-off everything from before. For the sun. For Australia.

Her sun-damaged skin. Caramel wrapping.

Three marriages.

A single marriage. Smashed-vases obstinacy.

Anorexia nervosa. Amid severe rations. Bombs. A legacy awoken two generations later.

School friends who went to France to their slaughter. A fiancé who never came back.

The Great Fog poisoning her baby's lungs.

Work. Telephone work. Office work. Factory work.

Her triple bypass. Her son's quadruple bypass. Her granddaughter, clutching her heart, eating tomatoes for their lycopene.

Religious conversions. More than one. Less than three.

Fatty mincemeat shepherd's pie. Peck's paste. Tuna boats. Corn relish on ham sandwiches. Rice salad. Canned asparagus. Bags of mixed nuts.

And grandfather. All I know of him was that he was poor, but not the poorest. The poorest didn't wear shoes to school. Before he died, Grandpa painted a self-portrait of his life, three metres long. A grand oil painting. Mum said that the image of his face as a dead man, at the bottom right corner, looked exactly as it did in the flesh, in his coffin. Waxy.

The other grandfather I know even less about.

She was gone, he said. She took him. And we were so young.

> —*Surely there were funny things too. Surely their lives were not pure sorrow.*

> —But—the narrative convenience of a sad story! Don't you feel it? Don't you feel sorry for the dead and all they endured?

> —*More compelling, right? The misery?*

> —The terrible things are the things she remembers being told. Behind the elders' backs.

—*Makes the past seem worth leaving behind. Worth forgetting.*

—Or worth writing about, silencing the slices of beauty and the slices of in-between.

She had animals, too. The cats, the rabbits. A rooster who liked to sit at the table when she hosted lunch parties. She was, after all, a fabulous hostess. Cooked elaborate dinner parties set in the dining room; lunches in the backyard. Everyone got drunk and screamed at each other.

Their friends were single people, gay people. Not family people. Theirs was not a house for children. An adult house with adult problems. Pieces of fine art and craft, porcelain, a French polish on the formal dining table. Every inch of the house stood frozen in terror of an invasion by children.

And she, far too austere for bacchanalian lunch parties. But she loved men. At least that was the phrase I heard. That was her pleasure.

She was thin and well-dressed even though there was no money to spare. An op-shop master. When someone asked her where her outfit came from, which was often, she'd say, 'Just a little boutique I know.' Each new man, each of her husbands, my mother once said, was a way of running from the last one—starting with her father.

She had her church, and later, her mosque. That part of her life is mysterious to me.

The third death. When the last person speaks your name.

All voted Labor.

The generation back are more fun. The words that are remembered. The twelve sisters. Half were beautiful. Half, heavy-set and stern. One was named Daisy. Or was it Eloise? All played the piano. Drank and gambled. Caused their husbands decadent grief. I love this gang of loose women whose genes I share a little in. The words I use to remember them are to me brilliant and pulsing with life, though they might describe a certain misery.

...

Writing in the first person is writing that admits that experience is always truncated. That perspective is necessarily incomplete. That it is not possible, not honest, to pretend otherwise. 'Point of view offers two possibilities: partial and complete,' writes Susan Stewart. Though the 'complete' view, the omnipotent view, the view that insists it knows everything, strikes me as a fearful perspective. A fear of what silence might reveal.

'What remains silent is the third and anonymous possibility,' Stewart says, is 'blindness, the end of writing'.

During the afternoons that I began to think about the book I was making from my life, I lay on my bed and read Kapil's *Ban en Banlieue*. Though reading it made me want to drown my book proposal and dissolve myself. In *Ban*, Kapil splices the lyric 'I', multiplies it, buries key fragments, and then undermines the composition of the very book in its own pages. She writes of:

the limits of the poetic project—its capacity: for embodiment, for figuration, for what happens to bodies when we link them to the time of the event...

These limitations ask, in turn, what kind of body constitutes an 'I'. It is a good question—what kind of body makes a memoir?

Certainly not the bodies of my grandmothers.

—*So what gives you the right?*

—Because she wanted to.

—Because I wanted to?

—Because she doesn't fear dying. Doesn't fear disappearing in time.

But the sadness the great sadness of everything being forgotten. Not only her moments. Not only her vision. But every image every pop song every name uttered every dense night and every morning the warm skin beside you before the day collapses inward. All of it, every shade of the light, gone. All at once.

—*She wanted to expunge herself.*

—What kind of body makes a memoir?

—'*Hey! I am going to make up an I that will stick to the pages of a book.*' (Kerry Sherin)

The one who does her homework. The one who cleans her plate. The one who drinks her soymilk. The one who falls face downwards. The one who high and mighty. The one of unspent honour.

The she of what next: action.

Books cited

Acker, Kathy. *Blood and Guts in High School*. Penguin Classics, 2017.

Acker, Kathy and McKenzie Wark. *I'm Very into You: Correspondence 1995–1996*. Semiotext(e)/Native Agents, 2015.

Adorno, Theodor. *Minima Moralia: Reflections from Damaged Life*. Verso, 2005.

Alexievich, Svetlana. *Zinky Boys: Soviet Voices from the Afghanistan War*. Translated by Robin and Julia Whitby. W. W. Norton & Company, 1992.

Bacon, Francis. *The Essays*. Penguin Classics, 1986.

Baker, Emerson. *A Storm of Witchcraft: The Salem Trials and the American Experience*. Oxford University Press, 2014.

Barthes, Roland. *Image—Music—Text*. Translated by Stephen Heath. Hill and Wang, 1977.

Boyer, Anne. *Garments Against Women*. Ahsahta Press, 2015.

—'The Consolations,' *Mirabilary*, Substack Newsletter, 2018.

Calvino, Italo. *Invisible Cities*. Translated by William Weaver. Vintage, 2002.

Carson, Anne. *Float*. Knopf, 2016.

—*Glass and God*. Jonathan Cape, 1998.

Catherine of Bologna. *The Seven Spiritual Weapons*. Translated by Hugh Feiss, OSB and Daniela Re. Wipf and Stock Publishers, 2011.

Chambers, Iain. *Migrancy, Culture, Identity*. Routledge, 1994.

Coleridge, Samuel Taylor. *Biographia Literaria: The Collected Works of Samuel Taylor Coleridge, Biographical Sketches of my Literary Life & Opinions (v. 7)*. Princeton UP, 1985.

Delany, Samuel R. *Shorter Views: Queer Thoughts & the Politics of the Paraliterary*. Wesleyan, 2011.

Dillard, Annie. *The Writing Life*. Harper Perennial, 1993.

Ernaux, Annie. *The Years*. Translated by Alison L. Strayer. Fitzcarraldo Editions, 2018.

Evans, Kate. *Red Rosa*. Verso, 2015.

Felman, Shoshana and Dori Laub. *Testimony: Crises of Witnessing in Literature, Psychoanalysis, and History*. Routledge, 1992.

Ferrante, Elena. *Frantumaglia: A Writer's Journey*. Translated by Ann Goldstein. Europa Editions, 2016.

Freud, Sigmund. 'Beyond the Pleasure Principle'. Edited by J. Rivkin and M. Ryan, *Literary Theory: An Anthology*. Blackwell Publishing, 2004.

Ginzburg, Natalia. *The Little Virtues*. Translated by Dick Davis. Arcade, 2013.

Glissant, Édouard. 'The Unforeseeable Diversity of the World'. Translated by Haun Saussy. Edited by Elisabeth Mudimbe-Boyi, *Beyond Dichotomies*. SUNY Press, 2002.

Handke, Peter. *A Sorrow Beyond Dreams*. Translated by Ralph Manheim. Pushkin Press, 2001.

Hardwick, Elizabeth. *Sleepless Nights*. New York Review Books, 2001.

Hemingway, Ernest. *A Moveable Feast*. Penguin Classics, 2012.

Heti, Shelia. *Motherhood*. Vintage, 2018.

Hodson, Chelsea. 'The Novel is Dead, Celebrity is a Disease, and More! Jarett Kobek Really Does Hate the Internet'. *Literary Hub*, February 2016.

Kapil, Bhanu. *Ban en Banlieu*. Nightboat Books, 2015.

—*The Vertical Interrogation of Strangers*. Kelsey Street Press, 2011.

Kincaid, Jamaica. *A Small Place*. Farrar, Straus and Giroux, 2000.

Kobek, Jarret. *I Hate the Internet*. We Heard You Like Books, 2016.

Kraus, Chris. *After Kathy Acker: A Biography*. Penguin Books, 2017.

—*I Love Dick*. Serpent's Tail, 2016.

Kristeva, Julia and Arthur Goldhammer. 'Stabat Mater'. *Poetics Today*, Volume 6, No. 1/2, The Female Body in Western Culture: Semiotic Perspectives, 1985.

Kristóf, Ágota. *The Notebook, The Proof, The Third Lie: Three Novels*. Translated by Alan Sheridan, Marc Romano and David Watson. Grove Press, 1997.

Li, Yiyun. *Dear Friend, from My Life I Write to You in Your Life*. Random House, 2017.

Liu, Alan. 'Time and the Literary'. Edited by Rita Felski, *Doing Time: Feminist Theory and Postmodern Culture*. New York UP, 2000.

Nelson, Maggie. *The Art of Cruelty: A Reckoning*. W. W. Norton & Company, 2011.

Proudhon, Pierre-Joseph. *Property Is Theft!: A Pierre-Joseph Proudhon Reader*. Edited by Iain McKay. AK Press, 2011.

Rankine, Claudia. *Don't Let Me Be Lonely.* Penguin Press, 2017.

Ruin, Hans. 'Life after Death'. Das Institut für die Wissenschaften vom Menschen, 2015.

Shakespeare, William. *Hamlet.* Edited by George Richard Hibbard. Oxford UP, 2008.

Sherin, Kerry. 'Guest Editor's Notes'. Edited by Juliana Spahr and Jena Osman, 'Chain: Memoir/Antimemoir'. University of Hawai'i, 2000.

Stein, Gertrude. *Selections.* Edited by Joan Retallack. University of California Press, 2008.

Stephens, Paul. *The Poetics of Information Overload: From Gertrude Stein to Conceptual Writing.* University of Minnesota Press, 2015.

Stewart, Susan. *On Longing: Narratives of the Miniature, the Gigantic, the Souvenir, the Collection.* Duke UP, 1993.

Tumarkin, Maria. *Traumascapes.* Melbourne University Publishing, 2005.

Weber, Max. *The Protestant Ethic and the Spirit of Capitalism.* Translated by Talcott Parsons. Routledge Classics, 2005.

Acknowledgments

In writing this book over several years, I have accrued many debts. Firstly, I owe deep gratitude to Alaina Gougoulis, Daisy Parente, Philip Gwyn Jones, Melinda Harvey, Jean Edelstein, and everyone at Text and Scribe UK, without whom a blueberry would just be a delicious, if costly, fruit. Heartfelt thanks to my friends who read and advised me: Dion Kagan, Maria Tumarkin, Ronnie Scott and Timothy Chandler.

I have referenced (stolen gratuitously from?) conversations, encounters and experiences with friends and strangers in this text. Credit here is due to Daniel Wright (RIP), Zübeyda Ahmed, Nader Ruhayel, Shasta Fisher, Natalie Costanzo, Natalie Briggs, Auntie Annie, Bhakthi Puvanenthiran, André Dao, Cat

McInnis, Otto Ivor, Ambika Trasi, Ahmed Awadalla, Yahia Saleh, Sammy Dunstan, Emma McNicol, Gene Flenady, Annabelle Stapleton-Crittenden, Tim Chandler (again), Stevie aka Robyn Delacroix, John Olstad, Detective Cristina Sereña, St Catherine of Bologna (RIP), Marianne Hirsch, Hans Ruin and a few men with names that remind me of 'Sam'. Others, too, whose names I don't remember.

Friends, colleagues and reference-letter writers who assisted this work in kind and sometimes abstract ways are Stephanie Van Schilt, Becky Harkins-Cross, Elena Gomez, Sam Cooney, Amy Gray, Eloise Grills, Oliver Reeson, Leah Jing, Adam Curley, Bronte Coates, Chris Somerville, Laura McPhee-Browne, Jen Nguyen, Rita Bullwinkel, Jessie Cole, Kate Callingham, Helen Garner, Robert Watkins, readers and subscribers of *Little Throbs*, and supporters of Synthetic Heat. Big thanks to Annabel Brady-Brown and Zoe Dzunko at the *Lifted Brow*, Sophie Allan at Chart Collective, Natalie Eilbert and Emily Raw at the *Atlas Review*, and Louise Swinn, editor of *Choice Words*.

My life and curiosity are the products of love and labour freely given by Mum, Dad, Jim, Rob, Sue and Emi. I composed parts of this text on unceded Wurundjeri land and I pay my respects to its rightful, traditional owners. I consumed groceries and paid bills while writing this with the material assistance of, variously, Australia Council for the Arts, Creative Victoria and an Australian Postgraduate Award. Romance and domestic collaboration was provided by Dominic Amerena, to whom I dedicate this book.